EDITOR IN CHIEF®

B1

GRAMMAR DISASTERS AND PUNCTUATION FAUX PAS

SERIES TITLES
Editor in Chief ®
Beginning
A1 ▪ A2
B1 ▪ B2
C1 ▪ C2

Created by Michael Baker

Written by Cheryl Block, Linda Borla,
Gaeir Dietrich & Margaret Hockett

Cover Design by Anna Allshouse
Illustrations by Kate Simon Huntley

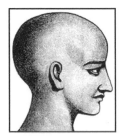

© 2000, 1995
THE CRITICAL THINKING CO.™
www.CriticalThinking.com
Phone: 800-458-4849 Fax: 831-393-3277
P.O. Box 1610 • Seaside • CA 93955-1610
ISBN 978-0-89455-516-9

TABLE OF CONTENTS

English consultant: Marc F. Bertonasco, Ph.D.
Professor of English
California State University Sacramento

To the Teacher

Objective

Editor in Chief® reinforces the rules of written English by providing the student with practice in editing a variety of formats. Students develop a basic understanding of the rules of grammar and mechanics in context and exercise their critical thinking abilities by identifying content errors. Books A1 and A2 cover the skills generally taught in Grades 4–6, books B1 and B2 cover skills taught in Grades 6–8, and books C1 and C2 cover skills for Grades 8 and up.

Rationale

The key difference between *Editor in Chief*® and most grammar series is the focus on editing in context. The grammatical and mechanical errors inserted into the activities are based on general instructional guidelines for specific grade levels; the content level, however, remains ungraded, allowing usage of these materials at many instructional levels. Styles and content are varied to sustain interest and broaden the student's exposure to different writing formats such as letters, directions, schedules, and dialogue. The illustrations integrated into the context of the activities further spark student interest. The editing skills developed can be applied to the student's own writing.

Activity

Each activity consists of 1–4 content errors (a discrepancy between the illustration/caption and the writing sample) and 6–12 errors in spelling, mechanics, and grammar. The student is asked to identify these errors and make the appropriate corrections. An editing checklist, included on page ix of this book, may be used by the student to aid in the editing task. Most corrections involve the insertion, modification, or deletion of punctuation marks, capitals, single words, and short phrases within the text. Each writing sample is based on an accompanying illustration and caption. Information in the illustration and caption is correct. (A content error occurs only where the story is contradicted by the illustration or caption.) The student may insert corrections and recopy the corrected article on the lines provided. Activities are sequenced according to the type, number, and level of errors included and the complexity of the subject matter.

Using the Answer Key

The answer key on pp. 35-57 lists corrections for each article. Each numbered error correction is followed by a shorthand explanation of the error type and a bracketed reference to the specific rules in the Grammar Guide on page 59. The teacher may choose to provide students with the number and type of errors prior to editing. In some instances, a student may be able to correct an error in more than one way. The answer key gives some obvious choices, but the teacher may choose to accept other answers that make sense and are grammatically and mechanically correct.

Teaching Suggestions

Editor in Chief® can be used as an individual or group activity for instruction, reinforcement, practice, and assessment of English grammar and mechanics. When a new rule is introduced, one article can serve as an instructional example and a second as an assessment of students' independent understanding. This book provides an excellent tool for authentic assessment of students' knowledge of grammar and mechanics. The Scope and Sequence on page vii gives teachers an overview of the types of errors included in each article, enabling them to individualize lessons more easily.

Suggested Uses for *Editor in Chief* ®

Regular Usage

- Group instruction—EIC® format is ideal for overhead projector.

- Cooperative learning—Students edit and exchange work to proofread.

- Homework—Individual activities can follow class instruction.

Extension Activities

- Students write their own paragraphs for editing.

- EIC® fosters class discussion of writing errors and how to avoid them.

- Editing checklist can be used to transfer editing skills to other writing activities.

Sources and Standards

In preparing this manuscript, we used the following references as standards for spelling, grammar, punctuation, and usage:

The American Heritage Dictionary, 3rd ed. (Boston: Houghton Mifflin Company, 1993).

The Chicago Manual of Style, 13th ed. (Chicago: The University of Chicago Press, 1982).

The Merriam-Webster Concise Handbook for Writers (Springfield, Mass.: Merriam-Webster Inc., 1991).

The Merriam-Webster Dictionary of English Usage (Springfield, Mass.: Merriam-Webster Inc., 1989).

The New York Public Library Writer's Guide to Style and Usage (New York: HarperCollins Publishers, Inc., 1994).

Warriner's English Grammar and Composition: Complete Course, Liberty Edition (Orlando: Harcourt Brace Jovanovich, 1986).

See sample *Reading Detective*® activity in back of book!

Scope and Sequence

TYPE OF ERROR	1	2	3	4	5	6	7	8	9	10	11	12	13	14	15	16	17	18	19	20	21	22	23	24	25	26	27	28	29	30	31	32	33
GRAMMAR/USAGE																																	
Adjective					■				■										■														
Adjec: comp./superl.		■	■									■							■							■		■	■				
Adverb						■										■					■							■					
Adverb: comp./superl.									■				■		■					■		■			■	■							
Agree: adjec./noun			■								■	■																■					
Agree: subject/verb	■		■		■		■	■	■	■	■		■		■	■									■	■	■			■			
Agree: pron./noun		■		■		■				■																		■		■			■
Article: a or an	■																	■															
Conjunction: correlat.																													■		■		
Double negative																										■							
Misplaced modifier															■					■						■							
Pronoun: subj./object							■									■		■	■		■	■				■			■	■	■	■	
Pronoun: possessive			■											■				■	■	■	■												
Pronoun: reflexive																																■	
Pronoun: first person				■																		■											
Subject: noun or pron.																																	
Tense: present/past												■	■	■		■		■						■		■		■					
Tense: future	■													■		■																	
Tense: perfect			■				■					■	■		■	■		■	■				■			■	■					■	
Usage																		■						■									
Verb: participle					■		■		■		■	■	■		■	■			■	■								■	■			■	
Verb: linking, helping			■					■				■				■		■	■			■					■						
Word pairs		■				■	■						■			■		■		■					■								
SPELLING	■	■	■	■		■			■			■	■	■				■	■	■			■	■	■		■			■			■
PUNCTUATION	1	2	3	4	5	6	7	8	9	10	11	12	13	14	15	16	17	18	19	20	21	22	23	24	25	26	27	28	29	30	31	32	33
Apostrophe: contrac.				■																■	■												
Apostrophe: possess.				■					■	■				■				■	■									■					
Colon							■											■								■							■
Comma: series													■																				
Comma: date/address																		■	■				■									■	■
Comma: introductory			■						■					■		■					■		■		■			■			■		
Comma: noun of address																		■														■	
Comma: interrupter																											■					■	
Comma: appositive					■								■										■									■	
Comma: coordin. conjunction										■				■	■	■				■	■		■	■		■		■					■
Comma: quotation						■	■									■											■		■				
Comma: letter																		■												■			■
Exclamation point							■																							■	■		
Hyphen																											■						■
Period: declarative																												■		■			■
Period: abbreviation				■			■						■																			■	
Run-on sentence		■					■	■							■		■													■	■		
Sentence fragment	■				■						■	■									■		■	■									
Question mark																						■	■			■					■	■	
Quotation marks									■						■	■							■				■	■		■		■	
CAPITALIZATION	1	2	3	4	5	6	7	8	9	10	11	12	13	14	15	16	17	18	19	20	21	22	23	24	25	26	27	28	29	30	31	32	33
First word of sentence										■																							
Proper noun							■				■								■				■		■	■					■		
Proper adjective		■		■	■																					■							
Title/abbreviation																	■	■					■		■								
In quotations				■	■									■																	■		■
Letter: opening, close																																■	
Day, month, holiday	■																■		■														

Styles and Topics

EXERCISE TITLE	WRITING STYLE	CONTENT: TOPIC	Fiction/ Nonfiction
1. The Planetarium	descriptive	Science: Astronomy	nonfiction
2. On a Grand Scale	expository	History: Egyptian pyramids	nonfiction
3. Uses of Peanut Oil	expository	Science: peanut oil	nonfiction
4. Predators Beware	narrative	Science: llamas	nonfiction
5. Mammal Discovery	expository	Science: new mammals	nonfiction
6. Camera Shy	narrative	Adventure: shark attack	fiction
7. Making Maple Syrup	descriptive	Farming: syrup	fiction
8. Time for Fun	narrative	Time Management: theme park	fiction
9. A Pirate's Life for Me?	descriptive	History: life of a pirate	nonfiction
10. Flying Mammals	expository	Science: bats	nonfiction
11. Fossil History	expository	Archaeology: timeline	nonfiction
12. Print Patterns	expository	Anatomy: fingerprints	nonfiction
13. On the Loose	narrative	Human Interest: tiger escape	fiction
14. A Note on the Trumpet	narrative	Music: trumpet	fiction
15. Let the Chips Fall	descriptive	How-to: recipe	fiction
16. Plane Scary	descriptive	Human Interest: air show	fiction
17. Pinto Show	descriptive (letter)	Human Interest: horse show	fiction
18. The Wright Stuff	expository	History: Wright Brothers	nonfiction
19. Wish You Were Here	descriptive	Travel: Polynesian Islands	fiction
20. Ride the Wild River	narrative	Sports: river rafting	fiction
21. Rash Results	descriptive	Science: poison oak	fiction
22. The Treasure Hunters	narrative	Recreation: treasure hunt	fiction
23. Venus's Flytrap	expository	Science: Venus's Flytrap	nonfiction
24. Birth of a Volcano	descriptive	Science: volcano	nonfiction
25. Stained Glass	descriptive dialog	Art: stained glass	fiction
26. Whale Watching Tours	descriptive	Human Interest: whale watching	fiction
27. The Gentle Sea Cow	expository	Science: manatee	nonfiction
28. Close Call	narrative	Human Interest: auto accident	fiction
29. Rescue	narrative	Human Interest: rescue	fiction
30. An Educational Trip	descriptive (letter)	Science: seaweed	fiction
31. Armchair Adventure	narrative dialog	Science: geysers	fiction
32. Mopping Up	narrative (letter)	Human Interest: housework	fiction
33. Letter to Madagascar	narrative (letter)	Science: lemurs	fiction

Editing Checklist

INSTRUCTIONS

The following list gives hints to help you find errors when editing. A word may be misspelled or used incorrectly. Punctuation and capitals may need to be inserted or removed. The caption and picture are always correct, but mistakes have been made in the story. You need to read carefully as you look for errors.

CAPITALIZATION Are the correct words capitalized? Do other words need capitals?	**CONTENT** Does the information in the paragraph match the caption and illustration?
GRAMMAR & USAGE	**PUNCTUATION**
Adjective or adverb: What kind of word does it modify? Is the correct form used?	**Apostrophe:** Is the word a contraction? Is the word a plural or possessive? Is the apostrophe in the right place?
Agreement: Does the verb agree with the subject? Does the pronoun agree with the noun it replaces? Does the adjective agree with the noun?	**Colon:** Is it used correctly? Is it placed correctly?
Articles: Do you use "a" or "an"?	**Comma:** Is it needed to separate words, dates, phrases, or clauses? Is it placed correctly?
Correlative conjunctions: Are either/or and neither/nor used correctly?	**Exclamation point:** Is it used correctly?
Misplaced modifier: Does the modifier make sense where it is placed within the sentence?	**Hyphen:** Is this a compound number?
Pronoun: Is it used as a subject or an object? Is the correct form used? Is first person last?	**Period:** Is it needed for a sentence or an abbreviation?
Usage: Is the correct word used? Does a word need to be changed?	**Run-on sentence:** Should this be more than one sentence?
Verb tense: Is the correct form used? Is a helping verb needed?	**Sentence fragment:** Is this a complete sentence?
Word pairs that are easily confused: Is the correct word used?	**Question mark:** Is the sentence or quotation a question? Is the question mark placed correctly?
SPELLING Are the words spelled correctly? Is the plural form correct?	**Quotation marks:** Is each part of a divided quotation enclosed? Are other punctuation marks placed correctly inside or outside the quotation marks? Is this a title of a song, chapter, etc.?

1. The Planetarium

You can expect light-years of travel during you're visit to a planetarium. Special lights that are shone on the flat sealing of the planetarium simulates the movements of the stars. Music and narration help set the mood. You can enjoy an view of the present night sky, or you can see how the stars appear in the future. On my first planetarium trip, I saw the Summer sky and many other scenes. My favorite was this view. From the Earth's surface.

In the planetarium, lights are shone on the curved ceiling to simulate stars and planets that may be light-years away. The author's favorite scene is shown above, where the Moon's craters surround the audience.

Find the 9 errors in this activity. There are no errors in the illustration or the caption.

_____

_____

_____

_____

_____

_____

2. On a Grand Scale

The ancient egyptian architects built on a grand scale. Their greatest achievement was the pyramids. These pyramids were constructed as tombs for the pharaohs, the base of the Great Pyramid near Cairo lays on a piece of land equal in size to ten football fields. Huge limestone blocks weighing as much as 500 pounds where placed layer upon layer to rise pyramids that were around 600 feet tall. Egyptian architects also built their structures to last. The three pyramids at Giza are the larger and best preserved of all the Egyptian pyramids. There over 4,000 years old. The pyramids are considered ones of the Seven Wonders of the Ancient World and are the only ones still standing.

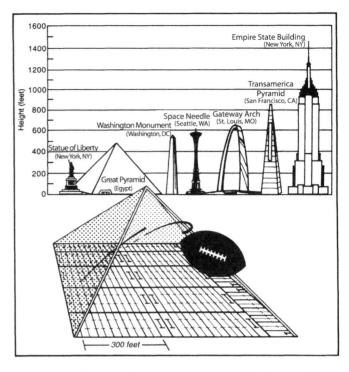

In comparison with many modern structures, the pyramids were relatively short in height but massive in volume. The base of the Great Pyramid, for example, covers ten football fields. Archaeologists can only theorize how the Egyptians, using limestone blocks weighing as much as 5,000 pounds, built the pyramids.

Find the 10 errors in this activity. There are no errors in the illustration or the caption.

_____

_____

_____

_____

_____

_____

3. Uses of Peanut Oil

Watch out if you having just eaten a peanut butter sandwich! That snack of your may be more powerful than you thinks. The oil of peanuts is used for making nitroglycerin, a nonexplosive ingredient of dynamite. The oil is rarely used in household items. Grooming products and paint sometimes contains peanut oil. It is used in salad dressing, to. Compared to olive oil, peanut oil is considered by some people to be the most tasty. Indeed peanut oil has many use.

Peanut oil is a common ingredient in many household items, including paint, grooming products, and salad dressing. It is also used to make nitroglycerin, the principal explosive ingredient of dynamite!

Find the 10 errors in this activity. There are no errors in the illustration or the caption.

_____

_____

_____

_____

_____

_____

4. Predators Beware

In south american countries, llamas are often used as pack animals. In the US, people are finding other uses for llamas. Some sheep ranchers use llamas to guard their flocks. Llamas graze in the fields with the sheeps and think of them as their herd. If the sheep are attacked, a llama will rush at the attacker and strike with their large hooves. It will also spit saliva into the attacker's face.

"Llamas are effective as the sheeps' protectors," says rancher Giselle Robinson, "Because they reduce the number of sheep lost to predators. Overall, Id say that we and llamas get along extremely well."

The llama is related to the camel. Llamas have no hooves but will use their large feet to attack the enemy. The llama above has just kicked a coyote that threatened the sheep herd.

Find the 9 errors in this activity. There are no errors in the illustration or the caption.

_____

_____

_____

_____

_____

_____

5. Mammal Discovery

In the early 1990s, scientists discovered two new species of mammals. Both was found in the isolated and mountainous Vu Quang Nature Reserve in Laos. The Vu Quang ox an ox which has long horns, is a distant relative of sheep and cattle. It was the first newly large mammal found in over 100 years. The giant muntjac, a deer with huge canine teeth, was discover soon after the Vu Quang deer. The first live specimen caught. Was a Vu Quang ox calf. It was sent to a Botanical garden in Hanoi for study.

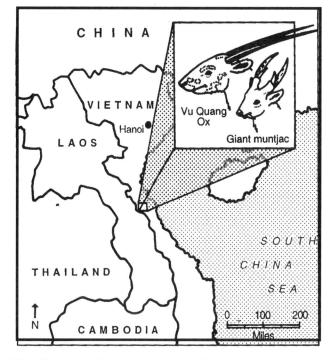

The first new large mammals discovered in over 50 years, the Vu Quang ox and the giant muntjac, were discovered in the Vu Quang Nature Reserve (see box in illustration) in the 1990s.

Find the 9 errors in this activity. There are no errors in the illustration or the caption.

_____

_____

_____

_____

_____

_____

6. Camera Shy

A tiger shark objected to having their photograph taken and sent two scuba divers swimming for cover. The divers, scientists with the National Oceanographic Society, were taking pictures for an upcoming article featuring the hammerhead's unique shaped head. After slowly circling the divers, the shark suddenly tried to butt them with it's head. Bob Noble, the diver armed with a rifle, made it into the diving cage first. Brian Block, the second diver, dropped both his camera and his tank as he swam to safety. Hammerhead sharks have been known to attack people, and the scientists were letting nothing to chance. "next time, we'll get his permission first" said the shaken Mr. Block.

Two divers are attacked while photographing a hammerhead shark. The diver armed with the shark dart makes it into the diving cage first. Although the second man loses two pieces of equipment, he saves his skin.

Find the 9 errors in this activity. There are no errors in the illustration or the caption.

_____

_____

_____

_____

_____

_____

7. Making Maple Syrup

Large sugar bush operators now have pipeline systems, but small farmers still gathers sap from sugar pine trees by hand they empty the sap into a big tub and drive it by tractor and wagon to the sugar shanty where the liquid is boiled. It takes about twenty-five gallons of sap to make one gallon of syrup

This year, Claire and Dave Bevy are looking for help. "Watch and learn from we experts", they say, "and you will do well. Then, if you ask permission to taste the sweet and sticky samples, our answer will be that you can. After a day of making maple syrup, you will be very tired, but you will have have a lot of fun"!

= 10 gallons of sap

In the sugar bush (grove of sugar maples), farmers tap the maple trees every spring in order to catch the running sap. The sap is boiled in a sugar shanty, or shack; it takes many gallons of sap to make one gallon of maple syrup!

Find the 9 errors in this activity. There are no errors in the illustration or the caption.

_____

_____

_____

_____

_____

_____

8. Time for Fun

We plan to see the shows while we is at Fun Park, Idaho. We notice on the schedule that the wild animal show will be given at 11;00 A.M. and 2:00 P.M. The bird show is in the large arena next to the animal show and was be presented at 10:00 AM. and 1:00 P.M. We really wants to see Wyatt's wild West Stunt Show on the other side of the park. We can see the animal show at 11:00 if we go to the stunt show at 10:00. Then we can take a break for lunch and go to the stunt show at 11:00 A.M. On the other hand, we can see the stunt show first, the bird show next, and the animal show last. Anyway, we will having seen them all by the day's end.

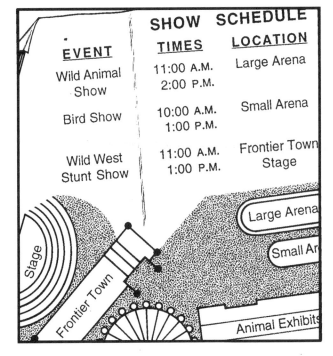

We expect to see all the shows at Fun Park and are using the schedule to organize our time.

Find the 10 errors in this activity. There are no errors in the illustration or the caption.

_____

_____

_____

_____

_____

_____

9. A Pirate's Life for Me?

"Yo ho, yo ho," it's a pirate's life for me." Pirate's lives were not as glamorous as books have portray them. Pirates made their living attacking merchant ships and inland towns the battles were brutal, and a pirate rarely lived long. Pirates were considered outlaws by all nations. They sailed under their own flag, the skull and crossbow, and lived by their own lose system of rules. These rules specified the share of the treasure each pirate received and the amount of compensation for lost limbs and other injuries. However very few of the pirates actually shared in the lavishly treasure chests of jewels and gold. Most was very poor, and many fared worst than beggars.

Pirates sailed under the skull and crossbones (a flag known as the Jolly Roger) and attacked merchant ships and towns along the North and South American coasts. In the Caribbean Sea alone, treasures worth millions of dollars lie buried beneath the waves.

Find the 11 errors in this activity. There are no errors in the illustration or the caption.

_____

_____

_____

_____

_____

_____

10. Flying Mammals

Bats are the only animals that can truly fly. Flying squirrels, and flying lemurs actually glide. Bats wings are formed by a membrane that stretches between the bones of their feet. The structure of birds' wings are different. A birds' wings are formed from the arm bones. Bats are nocturnal yet most have poor eyesight. This bats with poor eyesight use echolocation to guide their flights. they make supersonic sounds in their throats. They use the echoes from these sounds to guide itself and find food. Most echolocating birds actually catch small insects while flying in the air!

Bats are the only flying mammals. In flight, bats look much like birds, but unlike birds, bats' wings are formed from the bones of their hands. Also unlike birds, many bats use echolocation to guide themselves and find food even in total darkness!

Find the 11 errors in this activity. There are no errors in the illustration or the caption.

_____

_____

_____

_____

_____

11. Fossil History

Whom came first on earth? Was it the insects or the birds? A geologic time line can tell us. Geologists divide the earth's history into various units of time, and the greater unit of time is call an era. Our earliest fossil records of animal life on earth date back to the Cenozoic era. Insects appeared in the Paleozoic era and have remained unchanged for over 200 million years. The first birds, however, were toothless and appeared in the Mesozoic era during the Age of Fishes. An age be a time period used by biologists to indicate when one animal species are dominant. Modern toothless birds did not develop. Until the Cenozoic era. The earliest mammals appeared in the Mesozoic Era, but the Age of Mammals did not begin until 130 million years later in the Cenozoic era.

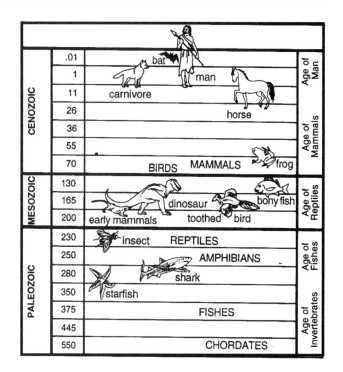

The geologic time line above covers the stages of development in animal life on earth. In geologic time, eras can be subdivided into epochs and periods. The three eras are named at left. Numbers refer to millions of years ago (the Age of Mammals began 70 million years ago).

Find the 10 errors in this activity. There are no errors in the illustration or the caption.

_____

_____

_____

_____

_____

_____

12. Print Patterns

Have you ever hear that no two fingerprints are alike? Each fingerprint is made up of a pattern of ridges. That vary in number, size, and location. They're are three basic patterns of fingerprints: loops, whirls, and arches. The more commonly occurring of the three pattern is the loop. A loop must have one ridge that enters from one side, curves around and exits from the opposite side. Whorls involve ridges that curve in a circular pattern. The arch the least common pattern is formed by ridges that enter from one side, rose in the middle, and then exit.

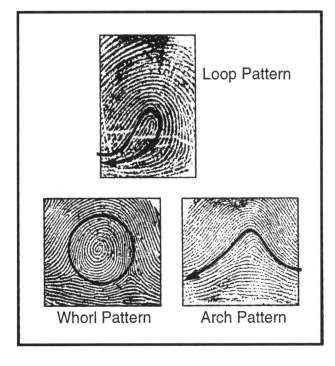

The three types of fingerprint patterns are the loop, the whorl, and the arch. The most common pattern, the loop, has a ridge that enters and exits from the same side.

Find the 10 errors in this activity. There are no errors in the illustration or the caption.

_____

_____

_____

_____

_____

13. On the Loose

Emmet Levison, zookeeper, recalls the days of transporting animals by train. "One time, a truck carrying a shipment of ours derailed and left thirty animals go free. Most of the beasts were rounded up, but an elusive lion had flee to a nearby back yard. After he was tranquilized, the big cat slump into a patch of berrys and could not even raise onto his feet." Emmet added that none of those animals was injured or lost, but the zoo administrator and he was worried. Emmet remembers saying, "the animals have tasted freedom, and we're not sure we may recapture them if this happens again."

It was an exciting day when this tiger escaped from a derailed train bound for the zoo and ended up in someone's back yard!

Find the 11 errors in this activity. There are no errors in the illustration or the caption.

_____

_____

_____

_____

_____

_____

14. A Note on the Trumpet

Hey I'm no slacker! I done some research when I started playing the trumpet. The early trumpet dates back to 2000 BC. That first trumpet was a lot different from my. It was probably made from a shell. It had no valves but players lended different qualities to they're tones by altering the shapes of their mouths. With todays trumpet, you can still play a lot of tones without pressing any of the valves. I myself have played a simple song this way. With four valves, though, I can play all of the notes in my range. I play an A using my first two valves, and I press just the third valve to play an F. With all the possible combinations, I'll betting I can play more well than those early trumpeters!

A trumpet has three valves, allowing the student to play all the notes within range. Here, the first and second valves are pressed to play the note A.

Find the 12 errors in this activity. There are no errors in the illustration or the caption.

_____

_____

_____

_____

_____

_____

15. Let the Chips Fall

Harold is get ready to bake a batch of cookies for Lisa to take to the carnival. He finds a recipe for peanut chip cookies, and reads it thoughtfully. Harold decide to add more chocolate chips and less flour so that the cookies will taste even better. He doubles the amount of chips and halves the flour. He puts 1/2 cup of flour into the bowl and adds the other dry ingredients. He carefully breaks and adds the three eggs and mixes in the remaining ingredients. He spoons the batter onto a greased cookie sheet and lies the sheet in the oven to bake for the required ten minutes. He takes the cookies out of the oven when the timer goes off the cookies are melted chocolate blobs. "Well, I can't send these to the carnival" says Harold, but they won't go to waste." He knows to who he will give the chocolate mass. "By tonight, Lisa will had tasted my new recipe for chocolate candy!"

CHOCOLATE CHIPPERS

2 c. flour   ½ c. butter
½ c. sugar   2 eggs
1 tsp. baking powder   ½ tsp. vanilla
1 cup chocolate chips

tsp. = teaspoon   Tbsp. = tablespoon   c. = cup

Mix dry ingredients together. Stir in & vanilla. Mix well. Add chocola...ased cookie she... spoon... at 350° for...

Harold uses the recipe above in his attempt to make chocolate chip cookies. He alters only the amounts of chocolate chips and flour.

Find the 12 errors in this activity. There are no errors in the illustration or the caption.

_____

_____

_____

_____

_____

_____

16. Plane Scary

The show at Blue Skies Airport was heavy clouded with smoke Saturday after Jan Fay's trimotor bursted into flames. As Fay fell toward the ground a parachute appeared over her fully opened head.

"The Federal Aviation Administration and the airport manager is reviewing the case," said investigator Lin. "The fact that we can't prevent air show disasters are very unfortunate. Jan Fay has flew for years, but piloting no longer interests her as much as constructing model airplanes. Next June, she will began her new hobby in earnest.

Jan Fay parachutes to safety as her flaming biplane hurtles to the earth during the Barnstormers Air Show on Sunday, May 5.

Find the 12 errors in this activity. There are no errors in the illustration or the caption.

17. Pinto Show

101 Pine St.
Westville NV 89500
July 8, 1994

Dear Nina

Please join me in Westville for the annual palamino show! It will be better than ever because chairman Pavick has planned a lot of new activities. When you come, take your partner so that you and him may compete in a mixed event. The pinto parade will be at 1200 on sunday, and a hour of various womens' and men's competitions will follow. The show runs for only four days Nina, so come as soon as you can.

Your friend,
Sula

The pinto show in Westville always takes place from the seventeenth to the twenty-first of July. Here is last year's photo of the pinto parade.

Find the 12 errors in this activity. There are no errors in the illustration or the caption.

18. The Wright Stuff

Many people know that on December 7, 1953 Orville and Wilbur Wright brung powered flight to humans. Other events in the Wright's lives may not be as well known. In the early years, the two sold bicycles. They could of continued in the bicycle business, but they developed an interest in aeronautics. They experimented with gliders and built a wing tunnel to test various wing shapes. For less than $100, the too men eventually designed and builded the first power airplane. Orville was the first to fly it because he have won a coin toss for the honor. It's hard to believe that their hometown newspaper did not even cover this momentous event in 1903, whom would have guessed that the skies would soon be our?

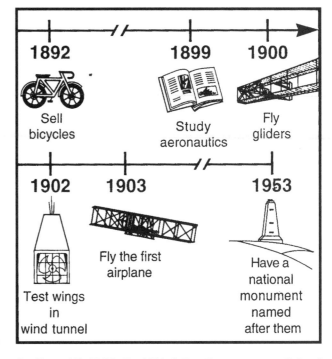

On Dec. 17, 1903, the Wright brothers accomplished sustained flight in the first power airplane (built for less than $1,000!). Though their achievements were not immediately recognized, the men were eventually honored when the Wright Brothers National Memorial was named.

Find the 13 errors in this activity. There are no errors in the illustration or the caption.

_____

_____

_____

_____

_____

19. Wish You Were Here

The Polynesian Islands have been a healthy change for Tia and me. We have a great view of the ocean and the palm trees from our tiled hut. Are favorite food here the coconut. The sweet fruit of a bush called the coconut palm.

Yesterday, auntie called from home and said, "Take me back some fresh coconuts. Ours best ones are not even as good as your baddest ones. Get them to Riley and I this spring." I'm afraid my aunt and uncle will have to wait until after spring. Even by june, Tia and I will not have spend enough time here!

Coconut palm trees surround our thatched hut on the ocean shore.

Find the 12 errors in this activity. There are no errors in the illustration or the caption.

_____

_____

_____

_____

_____

_____

20. Ride the Wild River

Rafting is a sport that appeals to the adventurous athlete. It's like a roller coaster ride without the seat belts. The beginning of our journey downriver was calm, and uneventful. We entered the rapids most abruptly than I had expected. The raft lifted by a wave and dropped into a pool of swirling water. The kayak spun around before the guide could point it back down river several times. Are oars were useless in the rushing water. We spent the rest of ours time bailing out all 20 feet of our raft as wave after wave came pouring over us. We were so wet and chilly that we were shake as we finally pulled into shore for the night. What an exhilarating day wed had!

Robert's Roaring Rapids River Tours offer several packages. A guide is provided on each raft, and no experience is required.

Find the 10 errors in this activity. There are no errors in the illustration or the caption.

_____

_____

_____

_____

_____

_____

21. Rash Results

In the Western woods don't be rash when you hike. You must watch out for poison oak. Madeleine Vu found this out the hard way while walking in Maine. "Poison oak is close related to poison ivy and has leaves made up of two leaflets. The plant contains an oil that causes a skin reaction. I could get poison oak not only through direct contact with the plant, but also through contact with anything the plants have touched. I could get it from mine dog or even my clothing. How would you like to be covered with itchy red spots like mine," Madeleine asks. "You may be sorry if you don't watch whats around you. Your rash will remind yourself for a very long time to be careful."

Madeleine Vu hikes in the California hills, where, after getting a bad case of poison oak, she has learned to avoid the distinctive triple leaflets.

Find the 9 errors in this activity. There are no errors in the illustration or the caption.

_____

_____

_____

_____

_____

_____

22. The Treasure Hunters

Carmen and Yoko had just read the story The Treasure Hunters in the bestselling book *Secrets of lost Treasures*. This morning, they wanted to play the board game with Anna and I.

"We'll play, I said, if you give me and Anna a head start of five squares."

"Well, okay," Carmen said. "Whose ready to start"

By 9:00, Carmen and Yoko have gotten there scuba gear, passed the danger zones, and landed four moves from the treasure chest entrance. It would have taken more than luck. For Anna and me to get out of Tank Creek and swipe the goods. We lost as expected. This was clearly our worse game ever played.

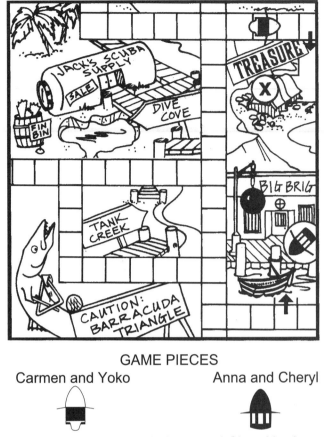

GAME PIECES

Carmen and Yoko   Anna and Cheryl

9:00 A.M.: Even though Anna and Cheryl had a 5-square head start, things are looking bad for them as they wait hopelessly in the brig (jail).

Find the 13 errors in this activity. There are no errors in the illustration or the caption.

_____

_____

_____

_____

_____

_____

23. Venus's Flytrap

Deep in the bogs of coastal north and south Dakota lurks an unusual plant the Venus's flytrap. The bogs provide damp soil, but the soil lacks the oxygen that the plant needs to survive. The Venus's flytrap has developed a unique way of getting this essential nutrient. Its hinged leafs have smooth edges, and sensitive hairs on the inside. When prey touches the hairs the leaf closes quickly. The struggling victim is trapped as the herbivorous plant secrets fluids to digest the insect and get the needed nitrogen.

The carnivorous Venus's Flytrap:
- Lives in coastal bogs in North and South Carolina.
- Has rounded, hinged leaves with bristled edges.
- Traps insects in its leaves.
- Secretes digestive fluids from leaves.
- Catches insects to get nitrogen, a nutrient the bogs lack.

Find the 11 errors in this activity. There are no errors in the illustration or the caption.

_____

_____

_____

_____

_____

_____

24. Birth of a Volcano

Imagine that you are walking through a corn field. The day is fine, but you our a bit nervous, because there have been a lot of earthquakes lately. Suddenly, a crack opens in the ground. And comes racing toward you. Steam rises from the crack and carries the smell of rotten eggs. You run away. Half an hour later you heard an explosion and see a black cloud rising high into the air. These events could of happened to you if you had been walking in the rice field 180 miles east of Mexico City, Mexico on January 20, 1943 when the volcano Parícutin was born.

The volcano Parícutin was born in a corn field 180 miles west of Mexico City on the 20th day of the second month of 1943. The eruption started with a crack opening and spewing forth steam and sulfur gas, which smelled like rotten eggs.

Find the 10 errors in this activity. There are no errors in the illustration or the caption.

_____

_____

_____

_____

_____

_____

25. Stained Glass

As visitors to a prominent window maker, we are honored to be given a tour by the owner. "At stained Panes, Inc.," president Cutler explains, "The art of constructing stained glass windows have been carefully preserved. Though our final products are made with special glass imported from Europe, we learn students to cut plain glass first. Would you like to watch one of our apprentices"? We look on as he say to the student, "For now, let's make a curved cut. You must apply pressure with the glass cutter as you roll it along a straight guide. Next, use the glass cutter to separate the two pieces of glass." Then Mr. Cutler says, "Next time, we'll try some curves. Of all the cutting jobs tight curves must be done the more careful. Stained glass is not an easy craft to perfect, but you will know it is worthwhile when you see the raising sun through a window of red and gold german glass."

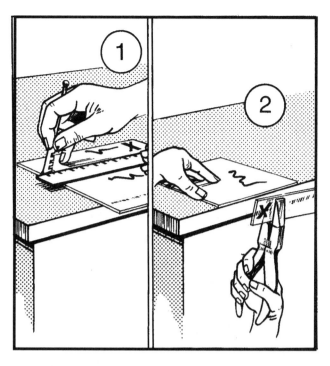

The student cuts a strip of glass. (1) She uses a glass cutter to make a straight score, or scratch. (2) She carefully separates the strip from the glass sheet by using a pair of glass pliers.

Find the 13 errors in this activity. There are no errors in the illustration or the caption.

_____

_____

_____

_____

_____

_____

26. Whale Watching Tours

Three cruise lines offer expeditions to see whales, but you should choose your sightseeing tour carefully. "The pilots for Poseidon's Passages," says dad, "run their boats the fast of all. If the rolling of the waves make you sick, you couldn't hardly get a badder ride." Many of my relatives agree. Some likes the Atlantis Cruises. Between you and myself, I think Fred's Fleet, my favorite, offers a great tour. You'll get a wonderful view of the whales as these acrobatic animals slice the water like knifes. Tours use to end at 600 P.M. but now there are late boats for evening passengers running at 7:00.

Frieda's Fleet, my personal favorite, now leaves every hour between 9:00 A.M. and 7:00 P.M. Here, whale-watching passengers look on as marine mammals perform.

Find the 13 errors in this activity. There are no errors in the illustration or the caption.

_____

_____

_____

_____

_____

_____

27. The Gentle Sea Cow

The manatee, or sea cow, be the only carnivorous mammal that lives entirely in the water. Manatees graze on underwater plants and can stay underwater for up to 45 minutes. The upper lip of the manatee are divided into two parts. It uses these two halves as pinchers to grab water plants. It can eat more than 1000 pounds of plants per day! The manatee likes cold coastal waters and, in the U.S., inhabits the bays and rivers of Florida. The gentle manatee is an endangered species. The encyclopedia article Sea Cows", in fact reports that one manatee, the Stellar's sea cow, was hunts to extinction twenty seven years after it was discovered!

The gentle, herbivorous manatee lives in warm coastal waters. Manatees can grow to be 14 feet long and weigh up to 1500 pounds. They can stay underwater for up to half an hour and eat more than 100 pounds of plants per day! In some parts of Florida and South America, manatees are used to keep waterways free of weeds.

Find the 11 errors in this activity. There are no errors in the illustration or the caption.

_____

_____

_____

_____

_____

_____

28. Close Call

Michael Farraday turned his convertible in too an oak tree on Forest Way while avoiding two deer. He said "that he had never saw animals appear so sudden. Michael had been listening to the tune Wild Nature when the two deer appeared out of nowhere. He describe the doe and then remark, "He and the fawn were the beautiful deers I've ever seen! I'll probably never encounter that two again, but I'll have a beauty of a dent to remind me of them."

A driver hit a pine tree after swerving to avoid a doe and her fawn crossing Forest Drive.

Find the 13 errors in this activity. There are no errors in the illustration or the caption.

_____

_____

_____

_____

_____

_____

29. Rescue

One spring day Jorge and his friend Antonio went hiking on Mt. Mateo. Jorge decided to take a route that looked more shorter than the trail, the slope he was climbing suddenly gave way, and Jorge was caught in a rock slide. He slid 50 feet, fell from a cliff that was 15 feet high, and came to rest on an inaccessible plateau. He had broke his leg and bruised his ribs. Jorge was unable to climb the rocky slope so he waited while Antonio went for help. Jorge was relieved when he looked to the east and saw the helicopter dropping him a lifeline. "It was quite an ordeal" Jorge said of the mens' experience. He added, "Him and me will stick closer to the trail next time".

After sliding down a rocky slope and falling 15 feet, Jorge landed a total of 75 feet from his starting point. Jorge waited for rescuers to fly in from the town in the tree-filled valley to the west.

Find the 12 errors in this activity. There are no errors in the illustration or the caption.

_____

_____

_____

_____

_____

_____

30. An Educational Trip

529 Evergreen Court
Boise, ID 83704
July 8, 1993

Dear Hiroshi.

My parents took my brother and myself to the seashore. Either my brother nor I had ever seen the ocean before. Wow. It was really great. There was seagulls all around the shore. We saw alot of plants and animals in the water, too. Did you know that there are many kinds of seaweeds. Seaweeds can be brown, red, or green. They are all algae, and they attach themself to sand and the part attached to the rocks is called a holdtight, and small animals live in it. Animals live on the leaves, too. One type of seaweed can grow a foot in a day, and some seaweeds grow to be very long. We saw a giant kelp that was green and almost 200 feet long!

Sincerely:
Basha

The rocky shore is home to many animals. It is also home to many kinds of seaweeds. Seaweeds can be brown, red, or green algae. Seaweeds attach themselves to rocks with a holdfast. Green algae do not grow as large as brown and red algae do. Giant kelp, a brown alga, can grow to be 200 feet long.

Find the 13 errors in this activity. There are no errors in the illustration or the caption.

_____

_____

_____

_____

_____

_____

31. Armchair Adventure

The article that Brandon is reading in *Adventure Travel* shows pictures from three areas in the world in which you can see geysers: Yellowstone National Park in Wyoming, Rotorua on the north island of New Zealand, and a site near Reykjavik, Iceland.

"Did you know that a geyser is like a pot bubbling over on the stove"? Brandon asked his sister. "Boiling water expands into steam, and the water and steam explode out of the geyser's mouth. It says here that minerals in the water can form cones or even towers around the mouth of a geyser"

"I already know all that," said Becky, "Because our Aunt has been to Yellowrock National Park, Wyoming with her husband."

"She went with who?" interrupted Brandon.

"She went with Uncle Earl," Becky said impatiently, and they also went to New Zealand and saw geysers right from their hotel room."

"Wow"! said Brandon. "Maybe they'll take you and myself next time."

He hoped to see the sights shown in the magazine she was reading. How about you? Would you like to see the places in "Hot Spots: Great Geysers of the World?"

Find the 12 errors in this activity. There are no errors in the illustration or the caption.

_____

_____

_____

_____

_____

_____

32. Mopping Up

35 Lawsome St
Jamesville, Iowa, 95832
August 13, 1985

dear Tonia,

Sam my roommate has been take the car to work. I've had to either take very short trips entertain me at home. I having found, however that lonely days are excellent for doing the housework. You should try it Tonia. This afternoon also happens to be good for writing letters. As you can see from my enclosed sketch, I haven't got much else to do until the living room floor dries.

your pal,
Jamal

9:00 A.M.: It's a good thing Jamal had a pencil and note paper in his pocket when he started waxing the floor at 8:30!

Find the 13 errors in this activity. There are no errors in the illustration or the caption.

_____

_____

_____

_____

_____

_____

33. Letter to Madagascar

University of Louisiana
Baton Rouge, LA 70803
April 29, 1994

Dr. Phillipe Tsirana
University of Madagascar
Antananarivo, Madagascar

Dear Dr. Tsirana,

Thank you for assisting me in obtaining a travel visa. I will arrive at 4:00 P.M. on June 6 and will stay for twenty six weeks to study the ring-tailed lemurs in their natural habitat. They live in the rain forest and woodland in southwestern Madagascar. My article will be titled "The impact of deforestation on territorial behavior in Ring-tailed Lemurs." I plan to bring my daughter with me. He is 14 and very excited about seeing Madagascar. I hope your colleague, Yvette, will be in town when we arrive. We look forward to seeing you and she. Oh I almost forgot. Whom will be meeting us at the airport and were should we meet?

Sincerely
Dr. Neva Ledesma

Each troop of 10 to 20 ring-tailed lemurs occupies its own territory in southwestern Madagascar and has little contact with other troops. Unlike other lemurs, ring-tailed lemurs spend most of their time on the ground. Dr. Ledesma is studying ring-tailed lemurs to see what effect, if any, deforestation is having on their territorial behavior.

Find the 12 errors in this activity. There are no errors in the illustration or the caption.

_____

_____

_____

_____

_____

_____

ANSWERS

This answer key provides the following information for each activity: the number and types of errors, a paragraph using superscribed numbers to show the locations of the errors, a corresponding number key explaining the errors, and the corrected paragraph.

Note that in the error count below, a run-on sentence or a sentence fragment is counted as one error even though the correction may require two changes, e.g., adding or deleting a period and a capital letter.

The errors in English mechanics in *Editor in Chief®* B1 have been geared to correspond to an intermediate-level English curriculum. For further information about the rules of grammar, usage, and punctuation covered in this book, see the Grammar Guide on pp. 59–83.

1. The Planetarium_____

9 errors—2 content; 1 capitalization; 3 grammar/usage; 1 punctuation; 2 spelling

The Planetarium Errors

You can expect light-years of travel during you're[1] visit to a planetarium. Special lights that are shone on the flat[2] sealing[3] of the planetarium simulates[4] the movements of the stars. Music and narration help set the mood. You can enjoy an[5] view of the present night sky, or you can see how the stars[6] appear in the future. On my first planetarium trip, I saw the Summer[7] sky and many other scenes. My favorite was this view. [8]From the Earth's[9] surface.

1. *your* visit—Spelling **[6.1]**
2. *curved*—Content: See illustration and caption **[2.1]**
3. *ceiling*—Spelling **[6.1]**
4. *simulate*—Usage: agreement of verb with subject (lights/simulate) **[4.2]**
5. *a* view—Grammar: article *a* before consonant sound **[3.5]**
6. *will* appear—Grammar: future tense **[3.24, 3.25]**
7. *summer*—Capital: unnecessary **[1.8]**
8. *view from*—Punctuation: sentence fragment **[5.38]**
9. *moon's*—Content: see illustration and caption (Earth appears in the background, so we cannot be viewing *from* the Earth; also, the caption says the moon's craters surround the audience.)
(Acceptable: view *of* the Earth's surface OR view *of* the Earth) **[2.1]**

The Planetarium Corrected

You can expect light-years of travel during your visit to a planetarium. Special lights that are shone on the curved ceiling of the planetarium simulate the movements of the stars. Music and narration help set the mood. You can enjoy a view of the present night sky, or you can see how the stars will appear in the future. On my first planetarium trip, I saw the summer sky and many other scenes. My favorite was this view from the Moon's surface.

2. On a Grand Scale _____

10 errors—2 content; 1 capitalization; 4 grammar/usage; 1 punctuation; 2 spelling

On a Grand Scale Errors

The ancient egyptian[1] architects built on a grand scale. Their greatest achievement was the pyramids. These pyramids were constructed as tombs for the pharaohs,[2] the base of the Great Pyramid near Cairo lays[3] on a piece of land equal in size to ten football fields. Huge limestone blocks weighing as much as 500[4] pounds where[5] placed layer upon layer to rise[6] pyramids that were around 600[7] feet tall. Egyptian architects also built their structures to last. The three pyramids at Giza are the larger[8] and best preserved of all the Egyptian pyramids. There[9] over 4,000 years old. The pyramids are considered ones[10] of the Seven Wonders of the Ancient World and are the only ones still standing.

1. *Egyptian* architects—Capital: proper adjective **[1.4]**
2. *pharaohs. The*—Punctuation: run-on sentence **[5.37, 1.1, 5.26]**
3. *lies* on—Usage: word pair (lie/lay) **[4.8]**
4. *5,000*—Content: see caption **[2.1]**
5. *were*—Spelling **[6.1]**
6. *raise* pyramids—Usage: word pair (rise/raise) **[4.8]**
7. *500* feet tall—Content: see illustration **[2.1]**
8. *largest*—Grammar: superlative adjective **[3.9, 3.1]**
9. *They're*—Spelling (Acceptable: *They are*) **[6.1]**
10. *one*—Usage: agreement of pronoun with noun (one of the Seven Wonders/ one) **[4.1]**

On a Grand Scale Corrected

The ancient Egyptian architects built on a grand scale. Their greatest achievement was the pyramids. These pyramids were constructed as tombs for the pharaohs. The base of the Great Pyramid near Cairo lies on a piece of land equal in size to ten football fields. Huge limestone blocks weighing as much as 5,000 pounds were placed layer upon layer to raise pyramids that were around 500 feet tall. Egyptian architects also built their structures to last. The three pyramids at Giza are the largest and best preserved of all the Egyptian pyramids. They're over 4,000 years old. The pyramids are considered one of the Seven Wonders of the Ancient World and are the only ones still standing.

3. Uses of Peanut Oil _____

10 errors—2 content; 6 grammar/usage; 1 punctuation; 1 spelling

Uses of Peanut Oil Errors

Watch out if you having[1] just eaten a peanut butter sandwich! That snack of your[2] may be more powerful than you thinks[3]. The oil of peanuts is used for making nitroglycerin, a nonexplosive[4] ingredient of dynamite. The oil is rarely[5] used in household items. Grooming products and paint sometimes contains[6] peanut oil. It is used in salad dressing, to[7]. Compared to olive oil, peanut oil is considered by some people to be the most[8] tasty. Indeed[9] peanut oil has many use[10].

1. *have* just eaten—Grammar: helping verb (used in present perfect tense) **[3.26, 3.24, 3.25]**
2. of *yours*—Grammar: possessive pronoun used without noun **[3.19]**
3. you *think*—Usage: agreement of verb with subject (in adverb clause) **[4.2]**
4. *an explosive*—Content: see caption **[2.1]**
5. oil is *commonly* used—Content: see illustration and caption (Acceptable: *often* OR *sometimes* OR *also* OR oil is ~~rarely~~ used) **[2.1]**
6. *contain*—Usage: agreement of verb with compound subject (products and paint/contain) **[4.3]**
7. *too*—Spelling **[6.1]**
8. *more* tasty—Grammar: comparative adjective **[3.9, 3.1]**
9. *Indeed,*—Punctuation: comma used after introductory word **[5.14]**
10. many *uses*—Usage: agreement of noun with adjective in number **[4.5]**

Uses of Peanut Oil Corrected

Watch out if you have just eaten a peanut butter sandwich! That snack of yours may be more powerful than you think. The oil of peanuts is used for making nitroglycerin, an explosive ingredient of dynamite. The oil is commonly used in household items.

Grooming products and paint sometimes contain peanut oil. It is used in salad dressing, too. Compared to olive oil, peanut oil is considered by some people to be the more tasty. Indeed, peanut oil has many uses.

4. Predators Beware _____

9 errors—1 content; 2 capitalization; 2 grammar/usage; 3 punctuation; 1 spelling

Predators Beware Errors

In south american[1] countries, llamas are often used as pack animals. In the US[2], people are finding other uses for llamas. Some sheep ranchers use llamas to guard their flocks. Llamas graze in the fields with the sheeps[3] and think of them as their herd. If the sheep are attacked, a llama will rush at the attacker and strike with their[4] large hooves[5]. It will also spit saliva into the attacker's face.

"Llamas are effective as the sheeps'[6] protectors," says rancher Giselle Robinson, "Because[7] they reduce the number of sheep lost to predators. Overall, Id[8] say that we and llamas[9] get along extremely well."

1. *South American*—Capital: proper adjective **[1.4]**
2. *U.S.,*—Punctuation: period after abbreviation **[5.27]**
3. *sheep*—Spelling (plural form) **[6.2]**
4. *its*—Usage: agreement of possessive pronoun with noun in number (a llama/its)
   (Acceptable: *his* large OR *her* large) **[4.1]**
5. *feet*—Content: see caption **[2.1]**
6. *sheep's* protectors—Punctuation: *'s* used with plural possessive not ending in *s* **[5.3]**
7. *"because*—Capital: unnecessary (divided quotation) **[1.2]**
8. *I'd* say—Punctuation: apostrophe used with contraction **[5.1]**
9. *llamas and we*—Grammar: first person last **[3.19]**

Predators Beware Corrected

In South American countries, llamas are often used as pack animals. In the U.S., people are finding other uses for llamas. Some sheep ranchers use llamas to guard their flocks. Llamas graze in the fields with the sheep and think of them as their herd. If the sheep are attacked, a llama will rush at the attacker and strike with its large feet. It will also spit saliva into the attacker's face.

"Llamas are effective as the sheep's protectors," says rancher Giselle Robinson, "because they reduce the number of sheep lost to predators. Overall, I'd say that llamas and we get along extremely well."

5. Mammal Discovery _____

9 errors—3 content; 1 capitalization; 3 grammar/usage; 2 punctuation

Mammal Discovery Errors

In the early 1990s, scientists discovered two new species of mammals. Both was[1] found in the isolated and mountainous Vu Quang Nature Reserve in Laos[2]. The Vu Quang ox[3] an ox which has long horns, is a distant relative of sheep and cattle. It was the first newly[4] large mammal found in over 100[5] years. The giant muntjac, a deer with huge canine teeth, was discover[6] soon after the Vu Quang deer[7]. The first live specimen caught. [8]Was a Vu Quang ox calf. It was sent to a Botanical[9] garden in Hanoi for study.

1. both *were*—Usage: agreement of verb with indefinite pronoun **[4.4]**
2. *Vietnam*—Content: see illustration and caption **[2.1]**
3. *ox,*—Punctuation: comma used with appositive **[5.16]**
4. *new* large mammal—Grammar: adjective modifies noun (new/mammal) **[3.1]**
5. *50*—Content: see caption **[2.1]**
6. was *discovered*—Grammar: past

participle (used in past tense passive voice) **[3.25, 3.24, 3.22]**

7. *ox*—Content: see caption **[2.1]**
8. *caught was*—Punctuation: sentence fragments **[5.38]**
9. *botanical*—Capital: unnecessary **[1.4]**

Mammal Discovery Corrected

In the early 1990s, scientists discovered two new species of mammals. Both were found in the isolated and mountainous Vu Quang Nature Reserve in Vietnam. The Vu Quang ox, an ox which has long horns, is a distant relative of sheep and cattle. It was the first new large mammal found in over 50 years. The giant muntjac, a deer with huge canine teeth, was discovered soon after the Vu Quang ox. The first live specimen caught was a Vu Quang ox calf. It was sent to a botanical garden in Hanoi for study.

6. Camera Shy_____

9 errors—3 content; 1 capitalization; 3 grammar/usage; 1 punctuation; 1 spelling

Camera Shy Errors

A tiger[1] shark objected to having their[2] photograph taken and sent two scuba divers swimming for cover. The divers, scientists with the National Oceanographic Society, were taking pictures for an upcoming article featuring the hammerhead's unique[3] shaped head. After slowly circling the divers, the shark suddenly tried to butt them with it's[4] head. Bob Noble, the diver armed with a rifle[5], made it into the diving cage first. Brian Block, the second diver, dropped both his camera and his tank[6] as he swam to safety. Hammerhead sharks have been known to attack people, and the scientists were letting[7] nothing to chance. "next[8] time, we'll get his permission first[9]" said the shaken Mr. Block.

1. *hammerhead*—Content: see picture and caption **[2.1]**
2. *its* photograph—Usage: agreement of pronoun with noun in number (shark/its)

(Acceptable: *his* photograph OR *her* photograph) **[4.1]**
3. *uniquely*—Grammar: adverb modifies adjective **[3.4]**
4. *its*—Spelling (possessive pronoun has no apostrophe) **[6.1]**
5. *shark dart*—Content: see caption **[2.1]**
6. *flipper*—Content: see illustration (Acceptable: *fin*) **[2.1]**
7. *leaving* nothing—Usage: word pair (leave/let) **[4.8]**
8. *"Next*—Capital: first word in quote **[1.2]**
9. *first,"*—Punctuation: comma separates quote from speaker (Acceptable: *first!"*) **[5.19]**

Camera Shy Corrected

A hammerhead shark objected to having its photograph taken and sent two scuba divers swimming for cover. The divers, scientists with the National Oceanographic Society, were taking pictures for an upcoming article featuring the hammerhead's uniquely shaped head. After slowly circling the divers, the shark suddenly tried to butt them with its head. Bob Noble, the diver armed with a shark dart, made it into the diving cage first. Brian Block, the second diver, dropped both his camera and his flipper as he swam to safety. Hammerhead sharks have been known to attack people, and the scientists were leaving nothing to chance. "Next time, we'll get his permission first," said the shaken Mr. Block.

7. Making Maple Syrup_____

9 errors—2 content; 4 grammar/usage; 3 punctuation

Making Maple Syrup Errors

Large sugar bush operators now have pipeline systems, but small farmers still gathers[1] sap from sugar pine[2] trees by hand[3] they empty the sap into a big tub and drive it by tractor and wagon to the sugar shanty where the liquid is boiled. It takes about twenty-five[4] gallons of sap to make one gallon of syrup.

This year, Claire and Dave Bevy are looking for help. "Watch and learn from we[5] experts",[6] they say, "and you will do well. Then, if you ask permission to taste the sweet and sticky samples, our answer will be that you can[7]. After a day of making maple syrup, you will be very tired, but you will have have[8] a lot of fun"![9]

1. farmers still *gather*—Usage: agreement of verb with subject (farmers/gather) **[4.2]**
2. from sugar *maple* trees—Content: see caption
   (Acceptable: from *maple* trees) **[2.1]**
3. *hand. They*—Punctuation: run-on sentence **[5.37, 5.26, 1.1]**
4. *forty*—Content: see diagram in illustration (using the key, multiply 4 buckets by 10 gallons per bucket to get 40 gallons of sap)
   (Acceptable: *twenty-five gallons of sap to make .625 gallon* OR *twenty-five gallons of sap to make 2/3 gallon*) **[2.1]**
5. *us* experts—Grammar: pronoun used as object **[3.19]**
6. *experts,"*—Punctuation: comma falls inside quotation marks **[5.20]**
7. *may*—Usage: word pair (may/can) **[4.8]**
8. will have *had*—Grammar: past participle (used in future perfect tense) **[3.25, 3.24, 3.22]**
9. *fun!"*—Punctuation: quoted exclamation **[5.24]**

Making Maple Syrup Corrected

Large sugar bush operators now have pipeline systems, but small farmers still gather sap from sugar maple trees by hand. They empty the sap into a big tub and drive it by tractor and wagon to the sugar shanty where the liquid is boiled. It takes about forty gallons of sap to make one gallon of syrup.

This year, Claire and Dave Bevy are

looking for help. "Watch and learn from us experts," they say, "and you will do well. Then, if you ask permission to taste the sweet and sticky samples, our answer will be that you may. After a day of making maple syrup, you will be very tired, but you will have had a lot of fun!"

8. Time for Fun_____

10 errors—3 content; 1 capitalization; 4 grammar/usage; 2 punctuation

Time for Fun Errors

We plan to see the shows while we is[1] at Fun Park, Idaho. We notice on the schedule that the wild animal show will be given at 11;00[2] A.M. and 2:00 P.M. The bird show is in the large[3] arena next to the animal show and was[4] be presented at 10:00 A[5]M. and 1:00 P.M. We really wants[6] to see Wyatt's wild[7] West Stunt Show on the other side of the park. We can see the animal show at 11:00 if we go to the stunt[8] show at 10:00. Then we can take a break for lunch and go to the stunt show at 11:00 A.M.[9] On the other hand, we can see the stunt show first, the bird show next, and the animal show last. Anyway, we will having[10] seen them all by the day's end.

1. *are*—Usage: agreement of verb with subject (in adverb clause) (we/are) **[4.2]**
2. *11:00* A.M.—Punctuation: colon used with hours and minutes **[5.4]**
3. *small*—Content: see illustration **[2.1]**
4. *will* be—Grammar: helping verb (used in future tense) **[3.26, 3.24]**
5. *A.M.*—Punctuation: period after abbreviation **[5.27]**
6. *want*—Usage: agreement of verb with subject (we/want) **[4.2]**
7. *Wild* West—Capital: proper noun **[1.3]**
8. *bird* show—Content: see illustration **[2.1]**
9. *1:00 P.M.*—Content: see illustration **[2.1]**

10. will *have* seen—Grammar: helping verb (used in future perfect tense) **[3.26, 3.24]**

Time for Fun Corrected

We plan to see the shows while we are at Fun Park, Idaho. We notice on the schedule that the wild animal show will be given at 11:00 A.M. and 2:00 P.M. The bird show is in the small arena next to the animal show and will be presented at 10:00 A.M. and 1:00 P.M. We really want to see Wyatt's Wild West Stunt Show on the other side of the park. We can see the animal show at 11:00 if we go to the bird show at 10:00. Then we can take a break for lunch and go to the stunt show at 1:00 P.M. On the other hand, we can see the stunt show first, the bird show next, and the animal show last. Anyway, we will have seen them all by the day's end.

9. A Pirate's Life for Me? _____

11 errors—2 content; 4 grammar/usage; 4 punctuation; 1 spelling

A Pirate's Life for Me? Errors

"Yo ho, yo ho,"[1] it's a pirate's life for me." Pirate's[2] lives were not as glamorous as books have portray[3] them. Pirates made their living attacking merchant ships and inland[4] towns [5]the battles were brutal, and a pirate rarely lived long. Pirates were considered outlaws by all nations. They sailed under their own flag, the skull and crossbow[6], and lived by their own lose[7] system of rules. These rules specified the share of the treasure each pirate received and the amount of compensation for lost limbs and other injuries. However[8] very few of the pirates actually shared in the lavishly[9] treasure chests of jewels and gold. Most was[10] very poor, and many fared worst[11] than beggars.

1. "Yo ho, yo *ho*, it's—Punctuation: unnecessary quotation marks (middle of quote) **[5.31]**
2. *Pirates'* lives—Punctuation: apostrophe used with plural

possessive ending in *s* **[5.3]**
3. have *portrayed*—Grammar: past participle (used in present perfect tense)
   (Acceptable: *as books portray them*) **[3.25, 3.24, 3.22]**
4. *coastal*—Content: see caption
   (Acceptable: ~~inland~~ towns *along the coast.*) **[2.1]**
5. *towns. The*—Punctuation: run-on sentence **[5.37, 5.26, 1.1]**
6. *crossbones*—Content: see caption
   (Acceptable: *flag, the Jolly Roger*) **[2.1]**
7. *loose*—Spelling **[6.1]**
8. *However,*—Punctuation: comma used after introductory word **[5.14]**
9. *lavish* treasure chests—Grammar: adjective modifies noun **[3.1]**
10. Most *were*—Usage: agreement of verb with indefinite pronoun **[4.4]**
11. fared *worse* than—Grammar: comparative adverb **[3.9]**

A Pirate's Life for Me? Corrected

"Yo ho, yo ho, it's a pirate's life for me." Pirates' lives were not as glamorous as books have portrayed them. Pirates made their living attacking merchant ships and coastal towns. The battles were brutal, and a pirate rarely lived long. Pirates were considered outlaws by all nations. They sailed under their own flag, the skull and crossbones, and lived by their own loose system of rules. These rules specified the share of the treasure each pirate received and the amount of compensation for lost limbs and other injuries. However, very few of the pirates actually shared in the lavish treasure chests of jewels and gold. Most were very poor, and many fared worse than beggars.

10. Flying Mammals _____

11 errors—3 content; 1 capitalization; 3 grammar/usage; 4 punctuation

Flying Mammals Errors

Bats are the only animals[1] that can

truly fly. Flying squirrels,[2] and flying lemurs actually glide. Bats[3] wings are formed by a membrane that stretches between the bones of their feet[4]. The structure of birds' wings are[5] different. A birds'[6] wings are formed from the arm bones. Bats are nocturnal[7] yet most have poor eyesight. This[8] bats with poor eyesight use echolocation to guide their flights. they[9] make supersonic sounds in their throats. They use the echoes from these sounds to guide itself[10] and find food. Most echolocating birds[11] actually catch small insects while flying in the air!

1. *mammals*—Content: see caption ("only flying mammals") [2.1]
2. *squirrels* and—Punctuation: unnecessary comma [5.21]
3. *Bats'* wings—Punctuation: apostrophe used with plural possessive [5.3]
4. *hands*—Content: see caption ("bones of their hands") [2.1]
5. wings *is*—Usage: agreement of verb with subject (structure/is) [4.2]
6. *bird's* wings—Punctuation: *'s* used with singular possessive [5.3]
7. *nocturnal,* yet—Punctuation: comma used before coordinating conjunction joining independent clauses [5.18, 5.33]
8. *These* bats—Usage: agreement of demonstrative adjective with noun [4.5]
9. *They*—Capital: first word in sentence [1.1]
10. *themselves*—Usage: agreement of pronoun with antecedent (They/themselves) [4.1]
11. echolocating *bats*—Content: see caption ("unlike birds, bats use echolocation") [2.1]

Flying Mammals Corrected

Bats are the only mammals that can truly fly. Flying squirrels and flying lemurs actually glide. Bats' wings are formed by a membrane that stretches between the bones of their hands. The structure of birds' wings is different. A bird's wings are formed from the arm bones. Bats are nocturnal, yet most have poor eyesight. These bats with poor eyesight use echolocation to guide their flights. They make supersonic sounds in their throats. They use the echoes from these sounds to guide themselves and find food. Most echolocating bats actually catch small insects while flying in the air!

11. Fossil History_____

10 errors—3 content; 1 capitalization; 5 grammar/usage; 1 punctuation

Fossil History Errors

Whom[1] came first on earth? Was it the insects or the birds? A geologic time line can tell us. Geologists divide the earth's history into various units of time, and the greater[2] unit of time is call[3] an era. Our earliest fossil records of animal life on earth date back to the Cenozoic[4] era. Insects appeared in the Paleozoic era and have remained unchanged for over 200 million years. The first birds, however, were toothless[5] and appeared in the Mesozoic era during the Age of Fishes[6]. An age be[7] a time period used by biologists to indicate when one animal species are[8] dominant. Modern toothless birds did not develop.[9] Until the Cenozoic era. The earliest mammals appeared in the Mesozoic Era[10], but the Age of Mammals did not begin until 130 million years later in the Cenozoic era.

1. *Who*—Grammar: pronoun *who* used as subject [3.21]
2. *greatest*—Grammar: superlative adjective [3.9]
3. is *called*—Grammar: past participle (used in present tense passive voice) [3.25, 3.24, 3.22]
4. *Paleozoic*—Content: see time line [2.1]
5. *toothed*—Content: see time line [2.1]
6. *Reptiles*—Content: see time line [2.1]
7. age *is* a time—Grammar: linking verb [3.27]
8. *is* dominant—Usage: agreement of verb with subject (in adverb clause)

(the subject, *species,* is singular)
(Acceptable: *was* dominant) **[4.2]**

9. *develop until*—Punctuation: sentence fragment **[5.38]**

10. *era*—Capital: unnecessary **[1.3]**

Fossil History Corrected

Who came first on earth? Was it the insects or the birds? A geologic time line can tell us. Geologists divide the earth's history into various units of time, and the greatest unit of time is called an era. Our earliest fossil records of animal life on earth date back to the Paleozoic era. Insects appeared in the Paleozoic era and have remained unchanged for over 200 million years. The first birds, however, were toothed and appeared in the Mesozoic era during the Age of Reptiles. An age is a time period used by biologists to indicate when one animal species is dominant. Modern toothless birds did not develop until the Cenozoic era. The earliest mammals appeared in the Mesozoic era, but the Age of Mammals did not begin until 130 million years later in the Cenozoic era.

12. Print Patterns _____

10 errors—2 content; 4 grammar/usage; 3 punctuation; 1 spelling

Print Patterns Errors

Have you ever hear[1] that no two fingerprints are alike? Each fingerprint is made up of a pattern of ridges.[2] That vary in number, size, and location. They're[3] are three basic patterns of fingerprints: loops, whirls[4], and arches. The more[5] commonly occurring of the three pattern[6] is the loop. A loop must have one ridge that enters from one side, curves around[7] and exits from the opposite[8] side. Whorls involve ridges that curve in a circular pattern. The arch[9] the least common pattern[9] is formed by ridges that enter from one side, rose[10] in the middle, and then exit.

1. Have you ever *heard*—Grammar: past participle (used in present perfect

tense) **[3.25, 3.24, 3.22]**

2. *ridges that* vary—Punctuation: sentence fragment **[5.38]**

3. *There are* three—Spelling (there/they're) **[6.1]**

4. *whorls*—Content: see caption **[2.1]**

5. *most* commonly—Grammar: superlative adverb **[3.9]**

6. three *patterns*—Usage: agreement of noun with adjective **[4.5]**

7. *around,* and—Punctuation: comma used after words in a series **[5.6]**

8. *same* side—Content: see caption **[2.1]**

9. *arch,* the least common *pattern,*—Punctuation: commas used with appositive **[5.16]**

10. *rise*—Grammar: present tense **[3.24, 3.22]**

Print Patterns Corrected

Have you ever heard that no two fingerprints are alike? Each fingerprint is made up of a pattern of ridges that vary in number, size, and location. There are three basic patterns of fingerprints: loops, whorls, and arches. The most commonly occurring of the three patterns is the loop. A loop must have one ridge that enters from one side, curves around, and exits from the same side. Whorls involve ridges that curve in a circular pattern. The arch, the least common pattern, is formed by ridges that enter from one side, rise in the middle, and then exit.

13. On the Loose _____

11 errors—2 content; 1 capitalization; 7 grammar/usage; 1 spelling

On the Loose Errors

Emmet Levison, zookeeper, recalls the days of transporting animals by train. "One time, a truck[1] carrying a shipment of ours derailed and left[2] thirty animals go free. Most of the beasts were rounded up, but an elusive lion[3] had flee[4] to a nearby back yard. After he was tranquilized, the big cat slump[5] into a patch of berrys[6] and could not even raise[7] onto his feet." Emmet added that none of those animals was[8] injured or lost, but the zoo administrator and he was[9] worried. Emmet remembers saying, "the[10] animals have tasted freedom, and we're not sure we may[11] recapture them if this happens again."

1. *train*—Content: see caption **[2.1]**
2. and *let*—Usage: word pair (let/leave) **[4.8]**
3. *tiger*—Content: see illustration and caption **[2.1]**
4. had *fled*—Grammar: past participle (used in past perfect tense) **[3.25, 3.24, 3.22]**
5. cat *slumped*—Grammar: past tense **[3.24, 3.22]**
6. *berries*—Spelling **[6.4]**
7. *rise*—Usage: word pair (rise/raise) **[4.8]**
8. *were*—Usage: agreement of verb with indefinite pronoun (none of those animals/were) **[4.4]**
9. *were*—Usage: agreement of verb with compound subject (administrator and he/were) **[4.3]**
10. *"The* animals—Capital: first word in direct quote **[1.2]**
11. *can*—Usage: word pair (can/may) **[4.8]**

On the Loose Corrected

Emmet Levison, zookeeper, recalls the days of transporting animals by train. "One time, a train carrying a shipment of ours derailed and let thirty animals go free. Most of the beasts were rounded up, but an elusive tiger had fled to a nearby back yard. After he was tranquilized, the big cat slumped into a patch of berries and could not even rise onto his feet." Emmet added that none of those animals were injured or lost, but the zoo administrator and he were worried. Emmet remembers saying, "The animals have tasted freedom, and we're not sure we can recapture them if this happens again."

14. A Note on the Trumpet _____

12 errors—2 content; 5 grammar/usage; 4 punctuation; 1 spelling

A Note on the Trumpet Errors

Hey[1] I'm no slacker! I done[2] some research when I started playing the trumpet. The early trumpet dates back to 2000 B[3]C. That first trumpet was a lot different from my[4]. It was probably made from a shell. It had no valves[5] but players lended[6] different qualities to they're[7] tones by altering the shapes of their mouths. With todays[8] trumpet, you can still play a lot of tones without pressing any of the valves. I myself have played a simple song this way. With four[9] valves, though, I can play all of the notes in my range. I play an A using my first two valves, and I press just the third[10] valve to play an F. With all the possible combinations, I'll betting[11] I can play more well[12] than those early trumpeters!

1. *Hey,*—Punctuation: comma used after interjection **[5.14]**
2. I *did*—Grammar: past tense (irregular) **[3.22, 3.24]**
3. 2000 B.C.—Punctuation: period used after abbreviation **[5.27]**
4. *mine*—Grammar: possessive pronoun used without noun (Acceptable: my *trumpet.*) **[3.19]**
5. *valves,* but—Punctuation: comma used before coordinating conjunction joining independent clauses **[5.18, 5.33]**
6. *lent*—Grammar: past tense (irregular) **[3.24, 3.22]**
7. *their*—Spelling **[6.1]**
8. *today's* trumpet—Punctuation: *'s* used with singular possessive **[5.3]**
9. *three* valves—Content: see illustration and caption **[2.1]**
10. *first* valve—Content: see illustration and caption **[2.1]**
11. I'll *bet*—Grammar: infinitive (used in future tense) **[3.22, 3.24]**
12. play *better* than—Grammar: comparative adverb **[3.9]**

A Note on the Trumpet Corrected

Hey, I'm no slacker! I did some research when I started playing the trumpet. The early trumpet dates back to 2000 B.C. That first trumpet was a lot different from mine. It was probably made from a shell. It had no valves, but players lent different qualities to their tones by altering the shapes of their mouths. With today's trumpet, you can still play a lot of tones without pressing any of the valves. I myself have played a simple song this way. With three valves, though, I can play all of the notes in my range. I play an A using my first two valves, and I press just the first valve to play an F. With all the possible combinations, I'll bet I can play better than those early trumpeters!

15. Let the Chips Fall _____

12 errors—3 content; 5 grammar/usage; 4 punctuation

Let the Chips Fall Errors

Harold is get[1] ready to bake a batch of cookies for Lisa to take to the carnival. He finds a recipe for peanut[2] chip cookies,[3] and reads it thoughtfully. Harold decide[4] to add more chocolate chips and less flour so that the cookies will taste even better. He doubles the amount of chips and halves the flour. He puts 1/2[5] cup of flour into the bowl and adds the other dry ingredients. He carefully breaks and adds the three[6] eggs and mixes in the remaining ingredients. He spoons the batter onto a greased cookie sheet and lies[7] the sheet in the oven to bake for the required ten minutes. He takes the cookies out of the oven when the timer goes off[8] the cookies are melted chocolate blobs. "Well, I can't send these to the carnival[9]" says Harold, [10]but they won't go to waste." He knows to who[11] he will give the chocolate mass. "By tonight, Lisa will had[12] tasted my new recipe for chocolate candy!"

1. is *getting*—Grammar: present participle (used in present progressive tense) **[3.25, 3.24, 3.22]**
2. *chocolate*—Content: see recipe in illustration **[2.1]**
3. *cookies* and—Punctuation: unnecessary comma **[5.21]**
4. Harold *decides*—Usage: agreement of verb with subject **[4.2]**
5. *one*—Content: see recipe in illustration **[2.1]** (Acceptable: *1*)
6. *two*—Content: see recipe in illustration and caption **[2.1]**
7. *lays* the sheet—Usage: word pair (lie/lay) **[4.8]**
8. *off. The*—Punctuation: run-on sentence (Acceptable: *off, and* the cookies) **[5.37, 5.26, 1.1]**
9. *carnival,"* says Harold,—Punctuation: comma separates quote from speaker **[5.19]**
10. *"but*—Punctuation: quotation marks enclose a divided quotation **[5.31]**
11. to *whom*—Grammar: pronoun *whom* used as object **[3.21]**
12. will *have* tasted—Grammar: helping verb (used in future perfect tense) (Acceptable: [although meaning changes] will *taste*) **[3.26, 3.24]**

Let the Chips Fall Corrected

Harold is getting ready to bake a batch of cookies for Lisa to take to the carnival. He finds a recipe for chocolate chip cookies and reads it thoughtfully. Harold decides to add more chocolate chips and less flour so that the cookies will taste even better. He doubles the amount of chips and halves the flour. He puts one cup of flour into the bowl and adds the other dry ingredients. He carefully breaks and adds the two eggs and mixes in the remaining ingredients. He spoons the batter onto a greased cookie sheet and lays the sheet in the oven to bake for the required ten minutes. He takes the cookies out of the oven when the timer goes off. The cookies are melted chocolate blobs. "Well, I can't send these to the carnival," says Harold, "but they won't go to waste." He knows to whom he will give the chocolate mass. "By tonight, Lisa will have tasted my new recipe for chocolate candy!"

16. Plane Scary _____

12 errors—2 content; 1 capitalization; 7 grammar/usage; 2 punctuation

Plane Scary Errors

The show at Blue Skies Airport was heavy[1] clouded with smoke Saturday[2] after Jan Fay's trimotor[3] bursted[4] into flames. As Fay fell toward the ground[5] a[6] parachute appeared over her fully opened[6] head.

"The Federal Aviation Administration and the airport manager is[7] reviewing the case," said investigator[8] Lin. "The fact that we can't prevent air show disasters are[9] very unfortunate.[10] Jan Fay has flew[11] for years, but piloting no longer interests her as much as constructing model airplanes. Next June, she will began[12] her new hobby in earnest.

1. *heavily*—Grammar: adverb modifies adjective **[3.4]**
2. *Sunday*—Content: see illustration and caption **[2.1]**
3. *biplane*—Content: see illustration and caption **[2.1]**
4. *burst*—Grammar: past tense (irregular) **[3.24, 3.22]**
5. *ground,* a—Punctuation: comma used after introductory dependent clause **[5.15]**
6. a *fully opened* parachute appeared over her head.—Usage: misplaced modifier
   (Acceptable: parachute *opened fully* ~~appeared~~ *over her* head OR parachute, *fully opened, appeared over her* head) **[4.6]**
7. Federal Aviation Administration and the airport manager *are* reviewing—Usage: agreement of verb with compound subject **[4.3]**
8. *Investigator* Lin—Capital: title used

as part of name **[1.6]**
9. *is*—Usage: agreement of verb with subject (fact/is) **[4.2]**
10. *unfortunate."*—Punctuation: quotation marks enclose a direct quote **[5.31]**
11. has *flown*—Grammar: past participle (used in present perfect tense) **[3.25, 3.24, 3.22]**
12. will *begin*—Grammar: infinitive (used in future tense) **[3.22, 3.24]**

Plane Scary Corrected

The show at Blue Skies Airport was heavily clouded with smoke Sunday after Jan Fay's biplane burst into flames. As Fay fell toward the ground, a fully opened parachute appeared over her head.

"The Federal Aviation Administration and the airport manager are reviewing the case," said Investigator Lin. "The fact that we can't prevent air show disasters is very unfortunate." Jan Fay has flown for years, but piloting no longer interests her as much as constructing model airplanes. Next June, she will begin her new hobby in earnest.

17. Pinto Show _____

12 errors—2 content; 2 capitalization; 3 grammar/usage; 5 punctuation

Pinto Show Errors

101 Pine St.
Westville[1] NV 89500
July 8, 1994

Dear Nina[2]

Please join me in Westville for the annual palamino[3] show! It will be better than ever because chairman[4] Pavick has planned a lot of new activities. When you come, take[5] your partner so that you and him[6] may compete in a mixed event. The pinto parade will be at 1200[7] on sunday[8], and a[9] hour of various womens'[10] and men's competitions will follow. The show runs for only four[11] days[12] Nina, so come as soon as you can.

Your friend,
Sula

1. *Westville,* NV—Punctuation: comma separates elements of address **[5.7]**
2. *Nina,*—Punctuation: comma used after greeting of friendly letter **[5.11]**
3. *pinto*—Content: see illustration and caption **[2.1]**
4. *Chairman* Pavick—Capital: title used as part of name **[1.6]**
5. *bring*—Usage: word pair (bring/take) **[4.8]**
6. *he*—Grammar: pronoun used as subject (in adverb clause) **[3.19]**
7. *12:00*—Punctuation: colon used with hours and minutes **[5.4]**
8. *Sunday*—Capital: day of week **[1.8]**
9. *an* hour—Grammar: article *an* before vowel sound **[3.5]**
10. *women's*—Punctuation: *'s* used with plural possessive not ending in *s* **[5.3]**
11. *five* days—Content: see illustration and caption (the 17th to the 21st is 5 days) **[2.1]**
12. *days,* Nina—Punctuation: comma used with noun of address **[5.13]**

Pinto Show Corrected

101 Pine St.
Westville, NV 89500
July 8, 1994

Dear Nina,

Please join me in Westville for the annual pinto show! It will be better than ever because Chairman Pavick has planned a lot of new activities. When you come, bring your partner so that you and he may compete in a mixed event. The pinto parade will be at 12:00 on Sunday, and an hour of various women's and men's competitions will follow. The show runs for only five days, Nina, so come as soon as you can.

Your friend,
Sula

18. The Wright Stuff_____

13 errors—3 content; 5 grammar/usage; 3 punctuation; 2 spelling

The Wright Stuff Errors

Many people know that on December 7,

1953[1, 2] Orville and Wilbur Wright brung[3] powered flight to humans. Other events in the Wright's[4] lives may not be as well known. In the early years, the two sold bicycles. They could of[5] continued in the bicycle business, but they developed an interest in aeronautics. They experimented with gliders and built a wing[6] tunnel to test various wing shapes. For less than $100[7], the too[8] men eventually designed and builded[9] the first power airplane. Orville was the first to fly it because he have[10] won a coin toss for the honor. It's hard to believe that their hometown newspaper did not even cover this momentous event[11] in 1903, whom[12] would have guessed that the skies would soon be our[13]?

1. *1903*—Content: see illustration **[2.1]**
2. *1903,*—Punctuation: comma used after year (month day, year,) in sentence **[5.10]**
3. *brought*—Grammar: past tense (irregular) **[3.22, 3.24]**
4. *Wrights'*—Punctuation: apostrophe used with plural possessive ending in *s* **[5.3]**
5. could *have*—Spelling **[6.5]**
6. *wind* tunnel—Content: see illustration **[2.1]**
7. *$1000*—Content: see caption **[2.1]**
8. *two*—Spelling **[6.1]**
9. *built*—Grammar: past tense (irregular) **[3.22, 3.24]**
10. *had* won—Grammar: helping verb (used in past perfect tense) **[3.26, 3.24]**
11. *event. In* 1903,—Punctuation: run-on sentence
    (Acceptable: *event! In* 1903, OR [though meaning changes slightly] *event in 1903. Who*) **[5.37, 5.26, 1.1]**
12. *who*—Grammar: pronoun *who* used as subject **[3.21]**
13. *ours*—Grammar: possessive pronoun used without noun **[3.19]**

The Wright Stuff Corrected

Many people know that on December 7, 1903, Orville and Wilbur Wright brought powered flight to humans. Other events in the Wrights' lives may not be as well known. In the early years, the two sold bicycles. They could have continued in the bicycle business, but they developed an interest in aeronautics. They experimented with gliders and built a wind tunnel to test various wing shapes. For less than $1000, the two men eventually designed and built the first power airplane. Orville was the first to fly it because he had won a coin toss for the honor. It's hard to believe that their hometown newspaper did not even cover this momentous event. In 1903, who would have guessed that the skies would soon be ours?

19. Wish You Were Here _____

12 errors—2 content; 2 capitalization; 6 grammar/usage; 1 punctuation; 1 spelling

Wish You Were Here Errors

The Polynesian Islands have been a healthy change for Tia and me. We have a great view of the ocean and the palm trees from our tiled[1] hut. Are[2] favorite food here [3]the coconut.[4] The sweet fruit of a bush[5] called the coconut palm.

Yesterday, auntie[6] called from home and said, "Take[7] me back some fresh coconuts. Ours[8] best ones are not even as good as your baddest[9] ones. Get them to Riley and I[10] this spring." I'm afraid my aunt and uncle will have to wait until after spring. Even by june[11], Tia and I will not have spend[12] enough time here!

1. *thatched* hut—Content: see illustration and caption **[2.1]**
2. *Our*—Spelling **[6.1]**
3. *is* the coconut—Grammar: linking verb
   (Acceptable: *here, the coconut, is the* sweet fruit) **[3.27]**
4. *coconut,* the—Punctuation: sentence fragment **[5.38]**
5. *tree*—Content: see illustration and caption **[2.1]**

6. *Auntie*—Capital: word used as proper name **[1.3]**
7. *Bring*—Usage: word pair (bring/take) **[4.8]**
8. *Our* best ones—Grammar: possessive pronoun used with noun **[3.19]**
9. *worst* ones—Grammar: superlative adjective **[3.9]**
10. Riley and *me*—Grammar: pronoun used as object **[3.19]**
11. *June*—Capital: month **[1.8]**
12. will not have *spent*—Grammar: past participle (used in future perfect tense) **[3.25, 3.24, 3.22]**

Wish You Were Here Corrected

The Polynesian Islands have been a healthy change for Tia and me. We have a great view of the ocean and the palm trees from our thatched hut. Our favorite food here is the coconut, the sweet fruit of a tree called the coconut palm.

Yesterday, Auntie called from home and said, "Bring me back some fresh coconuts. Our best ones are not even as good as your worst ones. Get them to Riley and me this spring." I'm afraid my aunt and uncle will have to wait until after spring. Even by June, Tia and I will not have spent enough time here!

20. Ride the Wild River _____

10 errors—2 content; 5 grammar/usage; 2 punctuation; 1 spelling

Ride the Wild River Errors

Rafting is a sport that appeals to the adventurous athlete. It's like a roller coaster ride without the seat belts. The beginning of our journey downriver was calm,[1] and uneventful. We entered the rapids most[2] abruptly than I had expected. The raft [3]lifted by a wave and dropped into a pool of swirling water. The kayak[4] spun around [5]before the guide could point it back down river several times[5]. Are[6] oars were useless in the rushing water. We spent the rest of ours[7] time bailing out all 20[8] feet of our raft as wave after wave came pouring over us. We were so wet and chilly that we were shake[9] as we finally pulled into shore for the night. What an exhilarating day wed[10] had!

1. *calm* and—Punctuation: unnecessary comma **[5.21]**
2. *more* abruptly—Grammar: comparative adverb **[3.9]**
3. *was* lifted—Grammar: helping verb (used in past tense passive voice) **[3.25, 3.26]**
4. *raft*—Content: see context and illustration (Acceptable: *It* spun) **[2.1]**
5. spun around *several times before*—Grammar: misplaced modifier **[4.6]**
6. *Our*—Spelling (*our* is possessive pronoun) **[6.1]**
7. *our* time—Grammar: possessive pronoun used with noun **[3.19]**
8. *13* feet—Content: see illustration **[2.1]**
9. were *shaking*—Grammar: present participle (used in past progressive tense) **[3.25, 3.24, 3.22]**
10. *we'd*—Punctuation: apostrophe used with contraction (Acceptable: *we had* had) **[5.1]**

Ride the Wild River Corrected

Rafting is a sport that appeals to the adventurous athlete. It's like a roller coaster ride without the seat belts. The beginning of our journey downriver was calm and uneventful. We entered the rapids more abruptly than I had expected. The raft was lifted by a wave and dropped into a pool of swirling water. The raft spun around several times before the guide could point it back downriver. Our oars were useless in the rushing water. We spent the rest of our time bailing out all 13 feet of our raft as wave after wave came pouring over us. We were so wet and chilly that we were shaking as we finally pulled into shore for the night. What an exhilarating day we'd had!

21. Rash Results

9 errors—2 content; 3 grammar/usage; 4 punctuation

Rash Results Errors

In the Western woods[1] don't be rash when you hike. You must watch out for poison oak. Madeleine Vu found this out the hard way while walking in Maine[2]. "Poison oak is close[3] related to poison ivy and has leaves made up of two[4] leaflets. The plant contains an oil that causes a skin reaction. I could get poison oak not only through direct contact with the plant,[5] but also through contact with anything the plants have touched. I could get it from mine[6] dog or even my clothing. How would you like to be covered with itchy red spots like mine,[7]" Madeleine asks. "You may be sorry if you don't watch whats[8] around you. Your rash will remind yourself[9] for a very long time to be careful."

1. *woods,*—Punctuation: comma used after introductory phrase **[5.15]**
2. *California*—Content: see caption **[2.1]**
3. *closely* related—Grammar: adverb modifies adjective **[3.4]**
4. *three* leaflets—Content: see illustration and caption **[2.1]**
5. *plant* but—Punctuation: unnecessary comma (in expressions contrasted through use of correlative conjunctions) **[3.11]**
6. *my* dog—Grammar: possessive pronoun used with noun **[3.19]**
7. *mine?"*—Punctuation: quoted question **[5.29, 5.30]**
8. *what's*—Punctuation: apostrophe used with contraction **[5.1]**
9. *you*—Grammar: pronoun used as object (not reflexive) **[3.20, 3.19]**

Rash Results Corrected

In the Western woods, don't be rash when you hike. You must watch out for poison oak. Madeleine Vu found this out the hard way while walking in California. "Poison oak is closely related to poison ivy and has leaves made up of three leaflets. The plant contains an oil that causes a skin reaction. I could get poison oak not only through direct contact with the plant but also through contact with anything the plants have touched. I could get it from my dog or even my clothing. How would you like to be covered with itchy red spots like mine?" Madeleine asks. "You may be sorry if you don't watch what's around you. Your rash will remind you for a very long time to be careful."

22. The Treasure Hunters _____

13 errors—2 content; 1 capitalization; 4 grammar/usage; 4 punctuation; 2 spelling

The Treasure Hunters Errors

Carmen and Yoko had just read the story [1]The Treasure Hunters[1] in the bestselling book *Secrets of [2]lost Treasures*. This morning, they wanted to play the board game with Anna and I[3].

"We'll play,[4] I said, [4]if you give me and Anna[5] a head start of five squares."

"Well, okay," Carmen said. "Whose[6] ready to start[7]"

By 9:00, Carmen and Yoko have[8] gotten there[9] scuba gear, passed the danger zones, and landed four[10] moves from the treasure chest entrance. It would have taken more than luck.[11] For Anna and me to get out of Tank Creek[12] and swipe the goods. We lost as expected. This was clearly our worse game ever played.[13]

1. *"The Treasure Hunters"*—Punctuation: quotation marks enclose story title **[5.32]**
2. *Secrets of Lost Treasures*—Capital: title of book **[1.9]**
3. Anna and *me*—Grammar: pronoun used as object **[3.19]**
4. *play,"* I said, *"if*— Punctuation: quotation marks enclose both parts of divided quotation **[5.31]**
5. *Anna and me*—Grammar: first person last **[3.19]**
6. *"Who's*—Spelling **[6.1]**

7. to *start?"*—Punctuation: quoted question **[5.29, 5.30]**
8. *had* gotten—Grammar: helping verb (used in past perfect tense) **[3.26, 3.24, 3.25]**
9. *their* scuba gear—Spelling (possessive pronoun) **[6.1]**
10. *two* moves—Content: see illustration **[2.1]**
11. *luck for*—Punctuation: sentence fragments **[5.38]**
12. *Big Brig*—Content: see illustration and caption
(Acceptable: *the Big Brig* OR *the brig* OR *jail*) **[2.1]**
13. *worst game*—Grammar: superlative adverb **[3.9]**

The Treasure Hunters Corrected

Carmen and Yoko had just read the story "The Treasure Hunters" in the bestselling book *Secrets of Lost Treasures*. This morning, they wanted to play the board game with Anna and me. "We'll play," I said, "if you give Anna and me a head start of five squares." "Well, okay," Carmen said. "Who's ready to start?" By 9:00, Carmen and Yoko had gotten their scuba gear, passed the danger zones, and landed two moves from the treasure chest entrance. It would have taken more than luck for Anna and me to get out of Big Brig and swipe the goods. We lost as expected. This was clearly our worst game ever played.

23. Venus's Flytrap _____

11 errors—4 content; 2 capitalization; 3 punctuation; 2 spelling

Venus's Flytrap Errors

Deep in the bogs of coastal north[1] and south[2] Dakota[3] lurks an unusual plant[4] the Venus's flytrap. The bogs provide damp soil, but the soil lacks the oxygen[5] that the plant needs to survive. The Venus's flytrap has developed a unique way of getting this essential nutrient. Its hinged leafs[6] have smooth[7] edges, [8] and sensitive hairs on the inside. When prey touches the hairs[9] the leaf closes quickly. The struggling victim is trapped as the herbivorous[10] plant secrets[11] fluids to digest the insect and get the needed nitrogen.

1. *North*—Capital: proper noun **[1.3]**
2. *South*—Capital: proper noun **[1.3]**
3. *Carolina*—Content: see caption **[2.1]**
4. *plant,*—Punctuation: comma used with appositive **[5.16]**
5. *nitrogen*—Content: see caption **[2.1]**
6. *leaves*—Spelling (plural of leaf) **[6.3]**
7. *bristled*—Content: see caption **[2.1]**
8. *edges* and—Punctuation: unnecessary comma **[5.21]**
9. *hairs,*—Punctuation: comma used after introductory dependent clause **[5.15]**
10. *carnivorous*—Content: see caption **[2.1]**
11. *secretes*—Spelling **[6.1]**

Venus's Flytrap Corrected

Deep in the bogs of coastal North and South Carolina lurks an unusual plant, the Venus's flytrap. The bogs provide damp soil, but the soil lacks the nitrogen that the plant needs to survive. The Venus's flytrap has developed a unique way of getting this essential nutrient. Its hinged leaves have bristled edges and sensitive hairs on the inside. When prey touches the hairs, the leaf closes quickly. The struggling victim is trapped as the carnivorous plant secretes fluids to digest the insect and get the needed nitrogen.

24. Birth of a Volcano _____

10 errors—3 content; 1 grammar/usage; 4 punctuation; 2 spelling

Birth of a Volcano Errors

Imagine that you are walking through a corn field. The day is fine, but you our[1] a bit nervous,[2] because there have been a lot of earthquakes lately. Suddenly, a crack opens in the ground.[3] And comes racing toward you. Steam rises from the crack and carries the smell of rotten eggs. You

run away. Half an hour later you heard[4] an explosion and see a black cloud rising high into the air. These events could of[5] happened to you if you had been walking in the rice field[6] 180 miles east[7] of Mexico City, Mexico[8] on January[9] 20, 1943[10] when the volcano Parícutin was born.

1. you *are*—Spelling (present tense verb) **[6.1]**
2. *nervous* because—Punctuation: unnecessary comma **[5.21]**
3. *ground and*—Punctuation: sentence fragment **[5.38]**
4. *hear*—Grammar: present tense **[3.24, 3.22]**
5. could *have*—Spelling **[6.5]**
6. *corn field*—Content: see illustration and caption **[2.1]**
7. *west*—Content: see caption **[2.1]**
8. *Mexico,* on—Punctuation: comma used after country in sentence **[5.8]**
9. *February*—Content: see caption ("second month") **[2.1]**
10. *1943,* when—Punctuation: comma used after year in sentence **[5.10]**

Birth of a Volcano Corrected

Imagine that you are walking through a corn field. The day is fine, but you are a bit nervous because there have been a lot of earthquakes lately. Suddenly, a crack opens in the ground and comes racing toward you. Steam rises from the crack and carries the smell of rotten eggs. You run away. Half an hour later you hear an explosion and see a black cloud rising high into the air. These events could have happened to you if you had been walking in the corn field 180 miles west of Mexico City, Mexico, on February 20, 1943, when the volcano Parícutin was born.

25. Stained Glass _____

13 errors—2 content; 4 capitalization; 5 grammar/usage; 2 punctuation

Stained Glass Errors

As visitors to a prominent window maker, we are honored to be given a tour by the owner. "At stained[1] Panes, Inc.," president[2] Cutler explains, "The[3] art of constructing stained glass windows have[4] been carefully preserved. Though our final products are made with special glass imported from Europe, we learn[5] students to cut plain glass first. Would you like to watch one of our apprentices"?[6] We look on as he say[7] to the student, "For now, let's make a curved[8] cut. You must apply pressure with the glass cutter as you roll it along a straight guide. Next, use the glass cutter[9] to separate the two pieces of glass." Then Mr. Cutler says, "Next time, we'll try some curves. Of all the cutting jobs[10] tight curves must be done the more careful[11]. Stained glass is not an easy craft to perfect, but you will know it is worthwhile when you see the raising[12] sun through a window of red and gold german[13] glass."

1. *Stained* Panes—Capital: proper noun **[1.3]**
2. *President* Cutler—Capital: title used as part of name **[1.6]**
3. *"the*—Capital: unnecessary (divided quotation) **[1.2]**
4. *has* been—Usage: agreement of verb with subject (art/has been) **[4.2]**
5. *teach*—Usage: word pair (teach/learn) **[4.8]**
6. *apprentices?"*—Punctuation: quoted question **[5.29]**
7. he *says*—Usage: agreement of verb with subject **[4.2]**
8. *straight*—Content: see illustration and caption **[2.1]**
9. *pliers*—Content: see caption **[2.1]**
10. *jobs,* tight—Punctuation: comma used after introductory phrase **[5.15]**
11. *most carefully*—Grammar: superlative adverb **[3.9]**
12. *rising*—Usage: word pair (rise/raise) **[4.8]**
13. *German*—Capital: proper adjective **[1.4]**

Stained Glass Corrected

As visitors to a prominent window maker, we are honored to be given a tour by the owner. "At Stained Panes, Inc.," President Cutler explains, "the art of constructing stained glass windows has been carefully preserved. Though our final products are made with special glass imported from Europe, we teach students to cut plain glass first. Would you like to watch one of our apprentices?" We look on as he says to the student, "For now, let's make a straight cut. You must apply pressure with the glass cutter as you roll it along a straight guide. Next, use the glass pliers to separate the two pieces of glass." Then Mr. Cutler says, "Next time, we'll try some curves. Of all the cutting jobs, tight curves must be done the most carefully. Stained glass is not an easy craft to perfect, but you will know it is worthwhile when you see the rising sun through a window of red and gold German glass."

26. Whale Watching Tours

13 errors—1 content; 1 capitalization; 8 grammar/usage; 2 punctuation; 1 spelling

Whale Watching Tours Errors

Three cruise lines offer expeditions to see whales, but you should choose your sightseeing tour carefully. "The pilots for Poseidon's Passages," says dad[1], "run their boats the fast[2] of all. If the rolling of the waves make[3] you sick, you couldn't[4] hardly get a badder[5] ride." Many of my relatives agree. Some likes[6] the Atlantis Cruises. Between you and myself[7], I think Fred's[8] Fleet, my favorite, offers a great tour. You'll get a wonderful view of the whales as these acrobatic animals slice the water like knifes[9]. Tours use[10] to end at 600[11] P.M.[12] but now there are late boats [13]for evening passengers running at 7:00[13].

1. *Dad*—Capital: word used as proper name **[1.7]**
2. *fastest*—Grammar: superlative adverb **[3.9]**

3. *makes*—Usage: agreement of verb with subject (feel/makes) **[4.2]**

4. *could* hardly—Usage: double negative (Acceptable: couldn't ~~hardly~~ get) **[4.7]**

5. *worse* ride—Grammar: comparative adjective **[3.9]**

6. Some *like*—Usage: agreement of verb with indefinite pronoun **[4.4]**

7. you and *me*—Grammar: pronoun used as object (not reflexive) **[3.20, 3.19]**

8. *Frieda's* Fleet—Content: see illustration and caption **[2.1]**

9. *knives*—Spelling (plural of knife) **[6.3]**

10. *used* to—Grammar: past tense **[3.24, 3.22]**

11. *6:00*—Punctuation: colon used with hours and minutes **[5.4]**

12. P.M., but—Punctuation: comma used before coordinating conjunction joining independent clauses **[5.18, 5.33]**

13. late boats *running at 7:00 for evening passengers.*—Usage: misplaced modifier
(Acceptable: but *now, for evening passengers, there are late boats running at 7:00.*) **[4.6]**

Whale Watching Tours Corrected

Three cruise lines offer expeditions to see whales, but you should choose your sightseeing tour carefully. "The pilots for Poseidon's Passages," says Dad, "run their boats the fastest of all. If the rolling of the waves makes you sick, you could hardly get a worse ride." Many of my relatives agree. Some like the Atlantis Cruises. Between you and me, I think Frieda's Fleet, my favorite, offers a great tour. You'll get a wonderful view of the whales as these acrobatic animals slice the water like knives. Tours used to end at 6:00 P.M., but now there are late boats running at 7:00 for evening passengers.

27. The Gentle Sea Cow _____

11 errors—4 content; 3 grammar/usage; 4 punctuation

The Gentle Sea Cow Errors

The manatee, or sea cow, be[1] the only carnivorous[2] mammal that lives entirely in the water. Manatees graze on underwater plants and can stay underwater for up to 45[3] minutes. The upper lip of the manatee are[4] divided into two parts. It uses these two halves as pinchers to grab water plants. It can eat more than 1000[5] pounds of plants per day! The manatee likes cold[6] coastal waters and, in the U.S., inhabits the bays and rivers of Florida. The gentle manatee is an endangered species. The encyclopedia article [7]Sea Cows",[8] in fact[9] reports that one manatee, the Stellar's sea cow, was hunts[10] to extinction twenty [11]seven years after it was discovered!

1. *is*—Grammar: linking verb **[3.27]**

2. *herbivorous*—Content: see caption **[2.1]**

3. *30* minutes—Content: see caption ("up to half an hour"; half an hour = 30 minutes)
(Acceptable: *one half hour* OR *1/2 hour*) **[2.1]**

4. *is*—Usage: agreement of verb with subject (lip/is) **[4.2]**

5. *100* pounds—Content: see caption **[2.1]**

6. *warm*—Content: see caption **[2.1]**

7. *"Sea Cows,"*—Punctuation: quotation marks enclose article title **[5.32]**

8. *"Sea Cows,"*—Punctuation: comma falls inside quotation marks **[5.20]**

9. in *fact,*—Punctuation: comma used with sentence interrupter **[5.17]**

10. was *hunted*—Grammar: past participle (used in past tense passive voice) **[3.25, 3.24, 3.22]**

11. *twenty-seven*—Punctuation: hyphen used in compound number **[5.25]**

The Gentle Sea Cow Corrected

The manatee, or sea cow, is the only herbivorous mammal that lives entirely in the water. Manatees graze on underwater plants and can stay underwater for up to 30 minutes. The upper lip of the manatee is divided into two parts. It uses these two halves as pinchers to grab water plants. It can eat more than 100 pounds of plants per day! The manatee likes warm coastal waters and, in the U.S., inhabits the bays and rivers of Florida. The gentle manatee is an endangered species. The encyclopedia article "Sea Cows," in fact, reports that one manatee, the Stellar's sea cow, was hunted to extinction twenty-seven years after it was discovered!

28. Close Call _____

13 errors—2 content; 7 grammar/usage; 2 punctuation; 2 spelling

Close Call Errors

Michael Farraday turned his convertible in too[1] an oak[2] tree on Forest Way[3] while avoiding two deer. He said "that[4] he had never saw[5] animals appear so sudden[6]. Michael had been listening to the tune [7]Wild Nature[7] when the two deer appeared out of nowhere. He describe[8] the doe and then remark[9], "He[10] and the fawn were the beautiful[11] deers[12] I've ever seen! I'll probably never encounter that[13] two again, but I'll have a beauty of a dent to remind me of them."

1. *into*—Spelling [6.1]
2. *a pine*—Content: see illustration and caption
   (Note that the article must change—*a* is used before a consonant sound.)
   [2.1]
3. Forest *Drive*—Content: see caption [2.1]
4. said *that*—Punctuation: unnecessary quotation marks (indirect quote) [5.31]
5. had never *seen*—Grammar: past participle (used in past perfect tense) [3.25, 3.24, 3.22]
6. *suddenly*—Grammar: adverb modifies verb [3.4]
7. *"Wild Nature"*—Punctuation: quotation marks enclose song title [5.32]

8. He *described*—Grammar: past tense [3.24, 3.22]
9. *remarked*—Grammar: past tense [3.24, 3.22]
10. *"She*—Usage: agreement of pronoun with noun in gender (doe [a female deer]/she) [4.1]
11. *most* beautiful—Grammar: superlative adjective [3.9]
12. *deer*—Spelling [6.2]
13. *those* two—Usage: agreement of demonstrative adjective with noun [4.5]

Close Call Corrected

Michael Farraday turned his convertible into a pine tree on Forest Drive while avoiding two deer. He said that he had never seen animals appear so suddenly. Michael had been listening to the tune "Wild Nature" when the two deer appeared out of nowhere. He described the doe and then remarked, "She and the fawn were the most beautiful deer I've ever seen! I'll probably never encounter those two again, but I'll have a beauty of a dent to remind me of them."

29. Rescue _____

12 errors—2 content; 4 grammar/usage; 6 punctuation

Rescue Errors

One spring day[1] Jorge and his friend Antonio went hiking on Mt. Mateo. Jorge decided to take a route that looked more[2] shorter than the trail,[3] the slope he was climbing suddenly gave way, and Jorge was caught in a rock slide. He slid 50[4] feet, fell from a cliff that was 15 feet high, and came to rest on an inaccessible plateau. He had broke[5] his leg and bruised his ribs. Jorge was unable to climb the rocky slope[6] so he waited while Antonio went for help. Jorge was relieved when he looked to the east[7] and saw the helicopter dropping him a lifeline. "It was quite an ordeal[8]" Jorge said of the mens'[9] experience. He added,

"Him[10] and me[11] will stick closer to the trail next time".[12]

1. *day,*—Punctuation: comma used after introductory phrase **[5.15]**

2. looked *shorter* than—Grammar: comparative adjective (Acceptable: looked *much* shorter) **[3.9]**

3. *trail. The*—Punctuation: run-on sentence **[5.37, 5.26, 1.1]**

4. *60* feet—Content: see caption (75 – 15 = 60) **[2.1]**

5. had *broken*—Grammar: past participle (used in past perfect tense) **[3.25, 3.24, 3.22]**

6. *slope,* so—Punctuation: comma used before coordinating conjunction joining independent clauses **[5.18, 5.33]**

7. *west*—Content: see illustration and caption (to see the helicopter, Jorge faces the valley, which lies to the west) **[2.1]**

8. *ordeal,"*—Punctuation: comma separates quote from speaker **[5.19]**

9. *men's*—Punctuation: *'s* used with plural possessive not ending in *s* **[5.3]**

10. *He*—Grammar: pronoun used as subject (Acceptable: *Antonio*) **[3.19]**

11. *I*—Grammar: pronoun used as subject **[3.19]**

12. *time."*—Punctuation: period inside quotation marks **[5.28]**

Rescue Corrected

One spring day, Jorge and his friend Antonio went hiking on Mt. Mateo. Jorge decided to take a route that looked shorter than the trail. The slope he was climbing suddenly gave way, and Jorge was caught in a rock slide. He slid 60 feet, fell from a cliff that was 15 feet high, and came to rest on an inaccessible plateau. He had broken his leg and bruised his ribs. Jorge was unable to climb the rocky slope, so he waited while Antonio went for help. Jorge was relieved when he looked to the west and saw the helicopter dropping him

a lifeline. "It was quite an ordeal," Jorge said of the men's experience. He added, "He and I will stick closer to the trail next time."

30. An Educational Trip _____

13 errors—3 content; 4 grammar/usage; 5 punctuation; 1 spelling

An Educational Trip Errors

529 Evergreen Court
Boise, ID 83704
July 8, 1993

Dear Hiroshi.[1]

My parents took my brother and myself[2] to the seashore. Either[3] my brother nor I had ever seen the ocean before. Wow.[4] It was really great. There was[5] seagulls all around the shore. We saw alot[6] of plants and animals in the water, too. Did you know that there are many kinds of seaweeds.[7] Seaweeds can be brown, red, or green. They are all algae, and they attach themself[8] to sand[9,10] and the part attached to the rocks is called a holdtight[11], and small animals live in it. Animals live on the leaves, too. One type of seaweed can grow a foot in a day, and some seaweeds grow to be very long. We saw a giant kelp that was green[12] and almost 200 feet long!

Sincerely:[13]
Basha

1. *Hiroshi,*—Punctuation: comma used after greeting of friendly letter **[5.11]**

2. my brother and *me*—Grammar: pronoun used as object (not reflexive) **[3.19, 3.20]**

3. *Neither*—Grammar: correlative conjunctions used in pairs (neither... nor) **[3.11]**

4. *Wow!*—Punctuation: interjection that stands alone (Acceptable: *Wow, it* was really *great*! OR *Wow!* It was really *great!*) **[5.23]**

5. There *were* seagulls—Grammar/usage: agreement of verb with subject (seagulls/were) **[4.2]**

6. *a lot*—Spelling **[6.5]**

7. *of seaweeds?*—Punctuation: question mark used after direct question **[5.29]**

8. *themselves*—Usage: agreement of pronoun (reflexive) with antecedent (they/themselves) **[4.1]**

9. to *rocks*—Content: see caption **[2.1]**

10. *rocks. The*—Punctuation: run-on sentence **[5.37, 5.26, 1.1]**

11. *holdfast*—Content: see caption **[2.1]**

12. *brown*—Content: see caption (giant kelp is a brown alga) **[2.1]**

13. *Sincerely,*—Punctuation: comma used after closing of letter **[5.12]**

An Educational Trip Corrected

529 Evergreen Court
Boise, ID 83704
July 8, 1993

Dear Hiroshi,

My parents took my brother and me to the seashore. Neither my brother nor I had ever seen the ocean before. Wow! It was really great. There were seagulls all around the shore. We saw a lot of plants and animals in the water, too. Did you know that there are many kinds of seaweeds? Seaweeds can be brown, red, or green. They are all algae, and they attach themselves to rocks. The part attached to the rocks is called a holdfast, and small animals live in it. Animals live on the leaves, too. One type of seaweed can grow a foot in a day, and some seaweeds grow to be very long. We saw a giant kelp that was brown and almost 200 feet long!

Sincerely,
Basha

31. Armchair Adventure_____

12 errors—2 content; 2 capitalization; 2 grammar/usage; 6 punctuation

Armchair Adventure Errors

"Did you know that a geyser is like a pot bubbling over on the stove"?[1] Brandon asked his sister. "Boiling water expands into steam, and the water and steam explode out of the geyser's mouth. It says here that minerals in the water can form cones or even towers around the mouth of a geyser[2]"

"I already know all that," said Becky, "Because[3] our Aunt[4] has been to Yellowrock[5] National Park, Wyoming[6] with her husband."

"She went with who[7]?" interrupted Brandon.

"She went with Uncle Earl," Becky said impatiently, [8]and they also went to New Zealand and saw geysers right from their hotel room."

"Wow"![9] said Brandon. "Maybe they'll take you and myself[10] next time."

He hoped to see the sights shown in the magazine she[11] was reading. How about you? Would you like to see the places in "Hot Spots: Great Geysers of the World?"[12]

1. *stove?"*—Punctuation: quoted question **[5.30]**

2. *geyser."*—Punctuation: period after quoted declarative sentence **[5.26, 5.28]**

3. *"because* our—Capital: unnecessary (divided quotation) **[1.2]**

4. our *aunt*—Capital: unnecessary (not used as proper name) **[1.3]**

5. *Yellowstone*—Content: see caption **[2.1]**

6. Park, *Wyoming,* with—Punctuation: comma used after state (city, state,) in sentence **[5.7]**

7. *whom?"*—Grammar: pronoun *whom* used as object **[3.21]**

8. impatiently, *"and*—Punctuation: quotation marks enclose both parts of divided quotation **[5.31]**

9. *"Wow!"*—Punctuation: quoted exclamation **[5.24, 5.23]**

10. take you and *me*—Grammar: pronoun used as object (not reflexive) **[3.20, 3.19]**

11. *he* was—Content: see caption (Brandon [he] was reading.) **[2.1]**

12. *World"?*—Punctuation: question mark used outside quotation marks when it doesn't apply to quoted material **[5.30]**

Armchair Adventure Corrected

"Did you know that a geyser is like a pot bubbling over on the stove?" Brandon asked his sister. "Boiling water expands into steam, and the water and steam explode out of the geyser's mouth. It says here that minerals in the water can form cones or even towers around the mouth of a geyser."

"I already know all that," said Becky, "because our aunt has been to Yellowstone National Park, Wyoming, with her husband."

"She went with whom?" interrupted Brandon.

"She went with Uncle Earl," Becky said impatiently, "and they also went to New Zealand and saw geysers right from their hotel room."

"Wow!" said Brandon. "Maybe they'll take you and me next time."

He hoped to see the sights shown in the magazine he was reading. How about you? Would you like to see the places in "Hot Spots: Great Geysers of the World"?

32. Mopping Up _____

13 errors—2 content; 2 capitalization; 4 grammar/usage; 5 punctuation

Mopping Up Errors

> 35 Lawsome St[1]
> Jamesville, Iowa,[2] 95832
> August 13, 1985

[3]dear Tonia,

Sam[4] my roommate[4] has been take[5] the car to work. I've had to either take very short trips [6]entertain me[7] at home. I having[8] found, however[9] that lonely days are excellent for doing the housework. You should try it[10] Tonia. This afternoon[11] also happens to be good for writing letters. As you can see from my enclosed sketch, I haven't got much else to do until the living room[12] floor dries.

> [13]your pal,
> Jamal

1. *St.*—Punctuation: period after abbreviation **[5.27]**
2. *Iowa*—Punctuation: unnecessary comma before ZIP code **[5.7]**
3. *Dear*—Capital: greeting of letter **[1.10]**
4. *Sam,* my *roommate,*—Punctuation: commas used with appositive **[5.16]**
5. has been *taking*—Grammar: present participle (used in present perfect progressive tense) **[3.25, 3.24, 3.22]**
6. *or* entertain—Grammar: correlative conjunctions used in pairs (either…or) **[3.11]**
7. *myself*—Grammar: reflexive pronoun **[3.20]**
8. *have* found—Grammar: helping verb (used in present perfect tense) (Acceptable: *am finding*) **[3.24, 3.26]**
9. *however,*—Punctuation: comma used with sentence interrupter **[5.17]**
10. *it,* Tonia.—Punctuation: comma used with noun of address **[5.13]**
11. *morning*—Content: see caption **[2.1]**
12. *kitchen*—Content: see illustration **[2.1]**
13. *Your*—Capital: closing of letter **[1.11]**

Mopping Up Corrected

> 35 Lawsome St.
> Jamesville, Iowa 95832
> August 13, 1985

Dear Tonia,

Sam, my roommate, has been taking the car to work. I've had to either take very short trips or entertain myself at home. I have found, however, that lonely days are excellent for doing the housework. You should try it, Tonia. This morning also happens to be good for writing letters. As you can see from my enclosed sketch, I haven't got much else to do until the kitchen floor dries.

> Your pal,
> Jamal

33. Letter to Madagascar _____

12 errors—1 content; 1 capitalization; 3 grammar/usage; 6 punctuation; 1 spelling

Letter to Madagascar Errors

University of Louisiana
Baton Rouge, LA 70803
April 29, 1994

Dr. Phillipe Tsirana
University of Madagascar
Antananarivo, Madagascar

Dear Dr. Tsirana,[1]
    Thank you for assisting me in obtaining a travel visa. I will arrive at 4:00 P.M. on June 6 and will stay for twenty six[2] weeks to study the ring-tailed lemurs in their natural habitat. They live in the [3]rain forest and woodland in southwestern Madagascar. My article will be titled "The [4]impact of deforestation on territorial behavior[4] in Ring-tailed Lemurs".[5] I plan to bring my daughter with me. He[6] is 14 and very excited about seeing Madagascar. I hope your colleague, Yvette, will be in town when we arrive. We look forward to seeing you and she[7]. Oh[8] I almost forgot. Whom[9] will be meeting us at the airport[10] and were[11] should we meet?

Sincerely[12]
Dr. Neva Ledesma

1. *Tsirana:*—Punctuation: colon used after greeting of a business letter [5.5]
2. *twenty-six*—Punctuation: hyphen used in compound number [5.25]
3. *thorn forest*—Content: see illustration and caption [2.1]
4. *"The Impact of Deforestation on Territorial Behavior in Ring-tailed Lemurs"*—Capital: title of article [1.9]
5. *Lemurs."*—Punctuation: period inside quotation marks [5.28]
6. *She* is—Usage: agreement of pronoun with noun in gender (daughter/she) [4.1]
7. you and *her*—Grammar: pronoun used as object [3.19]
8. *Oh,*—Punctuation: comma used after introductory word [5.14]
9. *Who* will—Grammar: pronoun *who* used as subject [3.19]

10. *airport,* and—Punctuation: comma used before coordinating conjunction joining independent clauses [5.18, 5.33]
11. *where*—Spelling [6.1]
12. *Sincerely,*—Punctuation: comma used after closing of a letter [5.12]

Letter to Madagascar Corrected

University of Louisiana
Baton Rouge, LA 70803
April 29, 1994

Dr. Phillipe Tsirana
University of Madagascar
Antananarivo, Madagascar

Dear Dr. Tsirana:
    Thank you for assisting me in obtaining a travel visa. I will arrive at 4:00 p.m. on June 6 and will stay for twenty-six weeks to study the ring-tailed lemurs in their natural habitat. They live in the thorn forest and woodland in southwestern Madagascar. My article will be titled "The Impact of Deforestation on Territorial Behavior in Ring-tailed Lemurs." I plan to bring my daughter with me. She is 14 and very excited about seeing Madagascar. I hope your colleague, Yvette, will be in town when we arrive. We look forward to seeing you and her. Oh, I almost forgot. Who will be meeting us at the airport, and where should we meet?

Sincerely,
Dr. Neva Ledesma

GUIDE TO GRAMMAR, USAGE, AND PUNCTUATION

The punctuation, grammar, and usage guidelines that follow cover all the skills used in this book. These skills represent a mid-level English curriculum. This guide is not meant to be a complete English reference. The types of errors are broken down into these areas: capitalization, content, grammar, usage, punctuation, and spelling. Specific topics are listed alphabetically under these main headings.

CAPITALIZATION

1.1   The first word in a sentence is capitalized.

> What a day we had!

1.2   Capitalize the first word in a direct quote. Do not capitalize a sentence fragment or the second half of a divided quotation.

> Jose said, "Come and look at the beautiful new mural on display in the library."
> "Come," Jose said, "and look at the beautiful new mural on display in the library."
> Jose said that he wanted us to see "the beautiful new mural."

1.3   Use a capital letter for a proper noun (not for a general noun). A proper noun names a specific person, place, or thing.

> Paris, France   the World Series   John Doe
>
> I go to Valley View <u>School</u>.   *but*   I go to the smaller <u>school</u>.

1.4   Use a capital letter for a proper adjective. A proper adjective is derived from a proper noun.

> African tribes   a Southern accent

1.5   Use a capital letter on the abbreviated forms of proper nouns and proper adjectives and initials.

> Nov. 27   U.C.L.A.

1.6   Use a capital letter on people's titles and their abbreviated forms only when they are used as part of a name or in place of a name.

> Captain John Smith   Capt. John Smith   John Smith was the captain.
>
> Doctor Susan White   Dr. Susan White   We saw the doctor.
>
> Yes, Captain, the lieutenant has left.   Oh, Doctor, I feel ill!

1.7   Capitalize words of familial relation when used in place of a name.

> At 1:00, Mother called us in for lunch.
>
> My mother called us in for lunch.

1.8   Capitalize the days of the week, the months, and the holidays. Do not capitalize a season unless it is being personified.

> Monday, December 24   New Year's Day   summer vacation
>
> as Winter grasped us in its chilly hands

1.9   Capitalize first and last words in the titles of books, songs, articles, poems, and movies. Capitalize all other words except articles, coordinating conjunctions, and prepositions of four or fewer letters (*in*, *the*, etc.).

> *Gone With the Wind*   *Men in Black*   "God Bless America"

1.10   Capitalize the greeting of a letter.

> Dear Julia,

1.11   Capitalize only the first word in the closing of a letter.

> Sincerely,   Yours truly,   Love,

CONTENT 2.1   In the *Editor in Chief* activities, any discrepancy between the title, illustration, or caption and the accompanying paragraph should be considered an error in the paragraph. Some content errors will be simple differences in information between an illustration/caption and the paragraph. Other content errors will require the student to analyze information from the illustration/caption in order to correct the paragraph.

GRAMMAR   Parts of Speech

Adjectives and Adverbs

Adjectives

3.1   Adjectives modify (give information about) nouns or pronouns. Adjectives tell what kind (*small* house), which one (*this* hat), or how many (*one* child). For more information, see the Usage section under Agreement: Adjective with Noun/Pronoun, 4.5.

3.2   The demonstrative adjectives *this* and *these* are used to indicate something that is nearby, while *that* and *those* are used to indicate something that is farther away.

> Nearby: *this* house, *these* houses

> Farther away: *that* house, *those* houses

3.3   Here and there are unnecessary with *this, that, these,* and *those.*

> Incorrect: this here box

> Correct: this box

See "Comparing and Contrasting Adjectives and Adverbs" on page 61 for more on using adjectives. See also "Demonstrative Pronouns" on page 65 for more on *this, that, these,* and *those.*

Adverbs

3.4   Adverbs modify verbs, adjectives, or other adverbs. Adverbs tell how, when, where, how often, how much, or to what extent. Regular adverbs are formed by adding *-ly* to an adjective; however, not all words that end in *-ly* are adverbs, and not all adverbs end in *-ly.*

> Example: She ran *quickly.* (quickly modifies verb—tells how she ran)

> Example: I swam *yesterday.* (yesterday modifies verb—tells when I swam)

> Example: He walked *downtown.* (downtown modifies verb—tells where he walked)

> Example: It is *very rarely* hot here. (very modifies adverb; rarely modifies adjective—together they tell how often it is hot)

> Example: That is an *extremely* beautiful apple. (extremely modifies adjective—tells to what extent the apple is beautiful)

See "Comparing and Contrasting Adjectives and Adverbs" on page 61 for more on using adverbs.

Articles

3.5   Articles (*a, an, the*) are adjectives. Use *an* before a vowel sound, *a* before a consonant sound. Confusion over which article to use most often comes with words beginning in *h*. If the word clearly begins with a vowel or consonant sound, the standard rule for articles applies. Confusion usually comes with words beginning with *h* in which the *h* is part of an unstressed or lightly stressed first syllable. In such cases, it is considered acceptable to use either *a* or *an*.

> Examples: an hour, a ham

> Examples: a historian or an historian, a heroic or an heroic

Comparing and Contrasting Adjectives and Adverbs

3.6   Most (but not all) adverbs end in *-ly*. Adjectives usually don't end in *-ly* (although a few do). Sometimes the same word functions as an adjective and an adverb. Sometimes adverbs of a particular word have more than one form. See the examples below.

Adjective	Adverb	Adverb ending in *-ly*
a *high* window	He leaped *high*.	We think *highly* of him.
a *close* encounter	He walked *close* to her.	We watched her *closely*.

Adjective ending in *-ly*	Adverb ending in *-ly*
nightly train	We go *nightly*.
lively tune	Step *lively*, boys!

These examples show that distinguishing between adverbs and adjectives is not as simple as checking to see whether a word ends in *-ly*. You need to see what the word modifies (describes).

Adjectives modify	Adverbs modify
nouns	verbs
pronouns	adjectives
	other adverbs

> Adjective: It rained *last* night. (*last* tells which night; it modifies the noun night)

> Adverb: Our team played *last*. (*last* tells when the team played; it modifies the verb played)

3.7   Linking verbs are frequently followed by adjectives.

> Adjective: She looked *pretty*. (*pretty* modifies the subject she)

> Adjective: He sounded *happy*. (*happy* modifies the subject he)

> Adjective: He felt *bad*. (*bad* modifies the subject he)

Many verbs that function as linking verbs can also be used as action verbs. In these cases, the action verbs will be followed by adverbs rather than adjectives.

> Linking verb with adjective: He stayed *quiet*. (*quiet* modifies the subject he)

> Action verb with adverb: He stayed *quietly* in his seat. (*quietly* modifies the verb stayed; it tells how he stayed in his seat)

Linking verbs take adjectives. Action verbs take adverbs. See "Linking Verbs" on page 71.

Well/Good

3.8   As modifiers, *well* and *good* are sometimes a source of confusion. *Well* is both an adverb and an adjective; *good* is only an adjective.

Perhaps some of the confusion comes because well and good occasionally overlap in meaning. You can say either "He feels well" or "He feels good" to indicate a general state of health. *Good* is not just limited to describing health, however. You can say "He feels good about his promotion." *Well* cannot be used in this way. As an adjective, *well* has only three meanings:

1. To be healthy.

   He looks *well*.

2. To look well-dressed or well-groomed.

   He looks *well* in a suit.

3. To be satisfactory, right, or proper.

   It is *well* to fulfill your commitments.

Good, on the other hand, is always an adjective. It cannot be used to modify a verb. In the examples below, *well* and *good* convey similar meanings, but they do so by modifying different types of words.

Good: You did a *good* job. (*good* is an adjective; it modifies job)

Well: You did *well*. (*well* is an adverb; it modifies did)

Another source of confusion may be that the comparative and superlative forms are the same for *good* and *well*: good, better, best and well, better, best. See below.

Comparative and Superlative Forms of Adjectives and Adverbs

3.9   Comparative and superlative forms of adjectives and adverbs are used to compare the degrees of characteristics possessed by the objects that they modify.

Most one-syllable adjectives/adverbs add the suffix *-er* or *-est* to the positive form.

hot—hotter—hottest small—smaller—smallest
lucky—luckier—luckiest

Some adjectives/adverbs use *more/most* to create the comparative and superlative forms.

quietly—more quietly—most quietly
beautiful—more beautiful—most beautiful

Less and least can also be used to create comparative and superlative forms.

aggressive—less aggressive—least aggressive
powerful—less powerful—least powerful

Irregular comparative forms

good/well—better—best

bad—worse—worst

many/much—more—most

Whether you use the comparative or superlative form (rather than the simple positive form) depends on how many things are being compared.

Comparative: The comparative form of adjectives and adverbs is used when comparing two items, two groups, or one item with a group.

He is the *older* of two children. (adjective)

The Jets are *better* than the Eagles. (adjective)

She runs *faster* than the boys. (adverb) *Note that she is not part of the boys.*

Superlative: The superlative form is used when comparing more than two things.

He is the *oldest* child of seven. (adjective)

The Jets are the sharpest of all the teams. (adjective)

She is the best player on the team. (adjective) *Note that she is part of the team.*

He sings the most beautifully. (adverb)

Conjunctions

The word *conjunction* refers to joining or coming together. We use conjunctions to join various grammatical elements: words, phrases, and clauses. There are three kinds of conjunctions: coordinating, correlative, and subordinating. Each of these three types of conjunctions is described below.

Coordinating Conjunctions

3.10   Coordinating conjunctions join words, phrases, clauses, or sentences. The word *coordinating* indicates that the elements that are joined have equal grammatical weight—for example, nouns with other nouns, verbs with other verbs, clauses with other clauses of equal rank. Another way to think of this is that coordinating conjunctions join constructions that are parallel.

He *ran and jumped.* (verb with verb)

We could use a new *car or truck.* (noun with noun)

I saw *two of my friends but none of my relatives* at the wedding. (2 phrases)

She had a new computer, so she took a class on home computing. (2 independent clauses)

There are seven coordinating conjunctions. To assist in remembering these conjunctions, use their first letters to form a mnemonic aid: FAN BOYS—**f**or, **a**nd, **n**or, **b**ut, **o**r, **y**et, **s**o.

When a coordinating conjunction joins two independent clauses, or main clauses, it should be preceded by a comma unless the independent clauses are short and closely related.

He came and he went.

We went to Paris, but we stayed only a few days.

Correlative Conjunctions

3.11   Correlative conjunctions is the name given to coordinating conjunctions used in pairs. The following are common correlative conjunctions:

either...or   neither...nor   both...and   not only...but (also)
whether...or

As with the other coordinating conjunctions, correlative conjunctions join elements of similar grammatical construction (e.g., two adjectives, two prepositional phrases, two independent clauses, etc.).

Correlative conjunctions should be placed as close as possible to the elements they join.

> Misplaced: Either *we will go to the lake* or *to the seashore.* (joins independent clause and prepositional phrase)

> Correct: We will go either *to the lake* or *to the seashore.* (joins 2 prepositional phrases)

In general, correlative conjunctions do not require commas; however, they may need a comma if they join two independent clauses. In the first example below, *not only…but* joins two independent clauses. In the second example, the same correlative conjunction joins two nouns (*cat* and *dog*).

> Not only do we have to wash the car, but we also must shampoo the carpets.

> We have not only a cat but also a dog.

Subordinating Conjunctions

3.12 Subordinating conjunctions join subordinate, or dependent, clauses to independent clauses. The following are commonly used subordinating conjunctions:

after	even though	than	wherever
although	how that	whether	
as	if though	while	
as if	in order that	unless	
as though	inasmuch as	until	
as much as	provided when		
because	since whenever		
before	so that where		

Anytime a subordinating conjunction begins a clause, that clause will be a subordinate clause. This is true even if the clause that follows the conjunction would otherwise be an independent clause.

> Independent clause: *we left the party*

> Subordinate clause: *after we left the party*

3.13 In general, when a sentence consists of a dependent clause followed by an independent clause, the dependent clause should be followed by a comma.

> Dependent clause + independent clause: After we left the party, we went for a walk.

> Dependent clause + independent clause: While the neighbors were away, the dog dug up the roses.

3.14 In general, when a dependent clause beginning with a subordinating conjunction follows an independent clause, no comma is required.

> Independent clause + dependent clause: We went for a walk after we left the party.

> Independent clause + dependent clause: The dog dug up the roses while the neighbors were away.

Beginning writers often insert commas before clauses beginning with the conjunctions *since* and *because. Since* and *because,* however, are subordinating, not coordinating, conjunctions. This means that even if *since* or *because* is followed by an independent clause, that clause is made subordinate by *since* or *because.* Such sentences containing *since* or *because* are examples of independent clauses + dependent clauses and do not require a comma.

> Example: We went right home from the store because we were afraid the ice cream would melt.

> Example: I wanted to ask him about the football game since I knew he had seen it.

For more on independent and dependent clauses, see "Clauses" on page 71 and "Clauses and Punctuation" on page 82.

Pronouns

Demonstrative Pronouns

3.15   When used alone (not modifying a noun), *this, that, these,* and *those* function as nouns and are considered demonstrative pronouns.

> *This* is a very nice rug.

> *Those* are pretty flowers.

In addition to identifying people or things, the demonstrative pronouns can be used to indicate spatial relationships.

> *This* is my house; *that* is my sister's. (This one is nearby; that one is farther away.)

Indefinite Pronouns

3.16   An indefinite pronoun does not refer to a specific person or thing. Some common indefinite pronouns are listed below.

all	everybody	no one
another	everyone	one
any	everything	other
anybody	few several	
anyone	many some	
anything	much somebody	
both	most someone	
each	neither something	
each one	nobody such	
either	none	

Indefinite pronouns are often used to make general statements or to indicate quantity.

> *Everybody* knows how upset she was.

> *Most* of the band members showed up for practice.

3.17   Unlike personal pronouns, indefinite pronouns use an apostrophe and *s* to form the possessive.

Everyone's cars got muddy after the storm.

He felt that *one's* actions should reflect *one's* beliefs.

3.18　　Note that if the indefinite pronoun is used as a possessive with *else*, *else* takes the apostrophe and *s*.

No one else's project looked as good as hers.

Personal Pronouns

3.19　　A personal pronoun replaces a noun or nouns. The pronoun must always agree in number and gender with the noun or nouns it replaces (see "Agreement: Pronoun with Antecedent," page 73). Pronouns may be used as subjects or objects in a sentence.

Subject: *We* children are hungry.

Object: Give some food to *us* children.

When a pronoun is used as the subject in a sentence, the verb must agree with the pronoun in number (see Agreement: Verb with Subject, page 73).

Pronouns may also show possession. A possessive pronoun may be used before a noun to show possession (*my* bike), or a possessive

SINGULAR/ PLURAL	PERSON	NOMINATIVE CASE (SUBJECT)	OBJECTIVE CASE (OBJECT)	POSSESSIVE CASE	
				BEFORE NOUN	STANDING ALONE
singular	first person	I	me	my	mine
singular	second person	you	you	your	yours
singular	third person	he	him	his	his
singular	third person	she	her	her	hers
singular	third person	it	it	its	its
plural	first person	we	us	our	ours
plural	second person	you	you	your	yours
plural	third person	they	them	their	theirs

pronoun may stand alone. (The bike is *mine*.) Note that unlike most nouns, possessive pronouns do not use an apostrophe to form the possessive.

Confusion in pronoun usage frequently occurs with compound subjects or objects (Marla and I, him and me). The easiest way to determine the correct form of the pronoun is to look at each member of the compound subject or object separately, as in these examples:

Marla and I went home. (*Marla* went home. *I* went home.)

Kim Lee went with him and me. (Kim Lee went with *him*. Kim Lee went with *me*.)

Bruce and he saw the movie. (*Bruce* saw the movie. *He* saw the movie.)

When the compound subject is broken apart in this way, most native speakers will recognize the correct pronoun form.

Note that the first person pronouns (I, me/we, us) always appear last in compound subjects and objects.

Reflexive and Intensive Pronouns

3.20   Reflexive and intensive pronouns use the same form. They are pronouns that end in *-self* or *-selves*: myself, yourself, herself, himself, itself, ourselves, yourselves, and themselves. They are used to refer to (reflexive) or emphasize (intensive) another noun or pronoun within the sentence.

Reflexive: A reflexive pronoun "reflects" back on an antecedent (the noun or pronoun to which it refers) that is within the same sentence.

>   Reflexive: I went by *myself*. (antecedent = I)

>   Reflexive: We could have done that *ourselves*. (antecedent = we)

Intensive: An intensive pronoun is used to emphasize or intensify an antecedent that is next to it within the same sentence.

Subject	Object	Possessive
who	whom	whose
whoever	whomever	whosever

>   Intensive: The girls *themselves* thought of the idea. (antecedent = the girls)

>   Intensive: You *yourself* may have seen something similar. (antecedent = you)

Note that both reflexive and intensive pronouns must have an antecedent that is within the same sentence. There is sometimes a tendency to use these pronouns incorrectly in place of personal pronouns.

>   Incorrect: She and *myself* went to the store after school. (no antecedent for *myself* in this sentence)

>   Correct: She and *I* went to the store after school.

>   Incorrect: He went with *myself*. (no antecedent for *myself* in this sentence)

>   Correct: He went with *me*.

Who and Whom

3.21   Who and whoever have three different forms depending upon their function in the sentence: subject, object, or possessive.

There is often a great deal of confusion over whether to use *who* or *whom*. If it functions as the subject, use *who*; if it functions as the object, use *whom*. The difficulty often lies in deciding whether you need a subject or object.

>   Subject: Who is coming for dinner?

>   Object: Whom are we waiting for?

The easiest way to decide whether to use *who* or *whom* (or *whoever* or *whomever*) is to mentally drop who/whom and the words preceding it and make a sentence with the words that are left by adding he or him. If you would use *he*, then the sentence needs a subject, and you should use *who*. If you would use *him*, then the sentence needs an object, and you should use *whom*. See the examples below.

>   Sentence: Do you know who/whom will be attending the meeting?

>   Remove who/whom: *will be attending the meeting*

Add he or him: *He* will be attending the meeting.

Correct: Do you know *who* will be attending the meeting?

Sentence: Who/whom is the party for?

Remove who/whom: *is the party for*

Add he or him: Is the party for *him*?

Correct: *Whom* is the party for?

Verbs

Verb Parts

3.22   All verbs have four principal parts: infinitive (sometimes called "plain verb"), present participle, past, and past participle. Present and past participles are used with helping verbs to form verb phrases. Regular verbs form the past and past participle by adding *-d* or *-ed* to the infinitive. Irregular verbs form the past and past participle forms in a different way, such as by changing spelling or by not changing at all.

Regular Verbs

Infinitive	Present Participle	Past	Past Participle
care	caring	cared	cared
call	calling	called	called
jump	jumping	jumped	jumped
walk	walking	walked	walked

Irregular Verbs

Infinitive	Present Participle	Past	Past Participle
bring	bringing	brought	brought
build	building	built	built
burst	bursting	burst	burst
choose	choosing	chose	chosen
do	doing	did	done
go	going	went	gone
lend	lending	lent	lent
ride	riding	rode	ridden
think	thinking	thought	thought
pay	paying	paid	paid
know	knowing	knew	known
shrink	shrinking	shrank	shrunk
		(or shrunk)	(or shrunken)

Verb Phrase

3.23   A verb phrase consists of a main verb and one or more helping verbs (also called auxiliary verbs). A few verb phrases are listed below:

Since many verb phrases are formed using the verb *to be*, we review its parts below:

Infinitive	Present Participle	Past	Past Participle
be	being	was, were	been

Verb Tense

3.24   Tense refers to the time element expressed by a verb. Verb tense shows whether an action has already occurred, is now occurring, or will occur in the future. Although there are four principal parts to verbs, these four parts are used to form six tenses: present tense, past tense, future tense, present perfect tense, past perfect tense, future perfect tense. These tenses can be subdivided into progressive form (be + present participle). Present and past can be further subdivided into emphatic.

Tense	Part of Verb Used	Example
present tense	Active: infinitive (Passive: be + past participle)	Active: I ask. (Passive: I am asked.)
present progressive	be + present participle	I am asking.
present emphatic	do + infinitive	I do ask.
present perfect tense	have or has + past participle	I have asked.
present perfect progressive	have or has + be (past participle) + present participle	I have been asking.
past tense	Active: past (Passive: be [past] and past participle)	Active: I asked. (Passive: I was asked.)
past progressive	be (past) + present participle	I was asking.
past emphatic	do (past) + infinitive	I did ask.
past perfect tense	had + past participle	I had asked.
past perfect progressive	had + be (past participle) + present participle	I had been asking.
future tense	Active: will or shall + infinitive (Passive: will or shall + be + past participle	Active: I will ask. (Passive: I will be asked.)
future progressive	will or shall + be (infinitive) + present participle	I will be asking.
future perfect tense	will (or shall) have + past participle	I will have asked.
future perfect progressive	will (or shall) have + be (past participle) + present participle	I will have been asking.

Irregular verb forms are sometimes confused. For example, in the verb *do*, the simple past tense *did* is sometimes incorrectly substituted for the past participle *done* in the perfect tenses. This results in *have did* (wrong) for *have done* (right). The past participles of both *do* and *go* are always used with a helping verb to create the present perfect, the past perfect, and the future perfect tenses.

Simple Past	Perfect tenses used with past participle		
did	have *done* (not did)	had *done*	will have *done*
went	have *gone* (not went)	had *gone*	will have *gone*

Participles

3.25   The present participle is used with a form of the verb *be* in the progressive tense. The form of *be* determines whether the sentence is present or past progressive.

Progressive = *be* + present participle

   Present progressive: The boy is flying a kite.

   Past progressive: The boy was flying a kite.

The past participle is used with a form of the verb *be* in passive voice. In passive voice, the subject of the sentence is being acted upon rather than acting.

Passive voice = *be* + past participle

   Passive voice (present): A kite is flown by the boy.

   Passive voice (past): A kite was flown by the boy.

Below are examples of active and passive voice in various tenses.

   Active (present): The dog chases the birds.

   Active (present perfect): The dog has chased the birds.

   Active (past): The dog chased the birds.

   Active (past perfect): The dog had chased the birds.

   Active (future): The dog will chase the birds.

   Active (future perfect): The dog will have chased the birds.

   Active (present progressive): The dog is chasing the birds.

   Active (present perfect progressive): The dog has been chasing the birds.

   Active (past progressive): The dog was chasing the birds.

   Active (past perfect progressive): The dog had been chasing the birds.

   Active (future progressive): The dog will be chasing the birds.

   Active (future perfect progressive): The dog will have been chasing the birds.

   Passive (present): The birds are chased by the dog.

   Passive (present perfect): The birds have been chased by the dog.

   Passive (past): The birds were chased by the dog.

   Passive (past perfect): The birds had been chased by the dog.

   Passive (future): The birds will be chased by the dog.

   Passive (future perfect): The birds will have been chased by the dog.

   Passive (present progressive): The birds are being chased by the dog.

   Passive (past progressive): The birds were being chased by the dog.

Helping Verbs

3.26   A helping verb (also called an auxiliary verb) is part of a verb phrase. A verb phrase consists of a main verb and a helping verb. Future tense, perfect tense, progressive form, and passive voice are all created using helping verbs.

Below are verb phrases with the helping verb marked in italics:

has written	*may* attend	*can* ski	*might have* seen
must read	*will* ride	*shall* go	*would have* taken

Common helping verbs include the following: be, can, could, do, have, may, might, must, shall, should, will, would.

Linking Verbs

3.27   Linking verbs express a state or condition rather than an action. They are called linking verbs because they link the subject to a complement which identifies or describes the subject. This subject complement may be a noun, pronoun, or adjective. Common linking verbs include the following: appear, be, become, feel, grow, look, remain, seem, smell, sound, stay, taste.

Anchovies *taste* salty.

That dog *looks* thin.

She *is* the manager.

Some linking verbs can also be used as action verbs, which can be modified by adverbs. A good way to determine whether the verb is functioning as a linking verb or action verb is to substitute the appropriate forms of *is* and *seem* for the verb. If the sentence still makes sense and has not changed its meaning, then the verb is a linking verb.

Linking verb: He remains happy. (No meaning change—He *is* happy. He *seems* happy.)

Action verb: He remains happily at the park. (Meaning changes—He *is* happily at the park. He *seems* happily at the park.)

Linking verbs take adjectives. Action verbs take adverbs.

Usage note: *Seem* is always a linking verb. When used as the main verb, *be* is a linking verb except when followed by an adverb. See "Comparing and Contrasting Adjectives and Adverbs" on page 61.

Parts of a Sentence

Clauses

All clauses contain a subject and a predicate. The fact that clauses have both a subject and a predicate distinguishes them from phrases (see "Phrases" page 72). Phrases may contain a subject or verb but not both.

Clauses are classified as to whether or not they make sense

standing alone. Clauses fall into two main categories: (1) clauses that make sense standing alone are called independent, or main, clauses and (2) clauses that do not make sense standing alone are called dependent, or subordinate, clauses.

Independent Clause/Main Clause

3.28   The terms *independent clause* and *main clause* can be used interchangeably. Independent, or main, clauses make sense standing alone. Adding an initial capital and ending punctuation transforms an independent clause into a simple sentence. Many sentences consist of nothing but an independent clause; however, a sentence may also contain one or more dependent clauses and even additional independent clauses.

Independent clause: it was a hot, humid day

Independent clause: I needed a cool drink

Two simple sentences: It was a hot, humid day. I needed a cool drink.

Note that by definition an independent clause is not a sentence. The terms *independent, or main, clause* and *sentence* refer to different levels of grammatical construction and cannot be used interchangeably. An independent clause is a group of words that represent a complete thought and contain a subject and verb. In addition, a sentence must begin with a capital letter and end with an appropriate punctuation mark.

Dependent Clause/Subordinate Clause

3.29   The terms *dependent clause* and *subordinate clause* can be used interchangeably. A subordinate, or dependent, clause does not represent a complete thought and cannot stand alone.

Dependent clause: where my brother had gone

Dependent clause: whom he was seeing

Dependent clauses must be combined with independent clauses in order to form sentences. In the sentences below, *we knew* and *we wondered* are independent clauses.

Simple sentence: We knew *where my brother had gone.*

Simple sentence: We wondered *whom he was seeing.*

For information on punctuating sentences containing independent and dependent clauses, see "Clauses and Punctuation" on page 81.

Phrases

3.30   In casual conversation, *phrase* refers to any group of words that function together. In the study of English, however, *phrase* has a more specific meaning, and we distinguish between phrases and clauses (see "Clauses" page 71). All groups of words that function together are either clauses (which contain both a subject and a verb) or nonclauses (which do not contain both a subject and a verb); nonclauses are phrases. So a phrase is a group of words that act as a unit and contain either a subject or a verb but not both.

Phrases may function as nouns, verbs, or modifiers. Phrases may be located anywhere in a sentence, but when they begin a sentence, they are usually followed by a comma. Phrases must always be part of a sentence. Like dependent clauses, phrases cannot stand alone. If a phrase is not part of a complete sentence, it is a sentence fragment.

Walking to the park was fun. (phrase functioning as a noun)

The dog *was running* quickly. (phrase functioning as a verb)

That is the prettiest flower *in the garden.* (phrase functioning as an adjective—modifies flower)

We went *to the mall.* (phrase functioning as an adverb—modifies went)

Phrases tend be confused with dependent clauses because neither of them forms a complete thought. Remember, a clause will have both a subject and a verb, and a phrase will have one or the other but not both.

Subject

3.31   Subject: Use a noun or pronoun (not both) as subject.

Incorrect: Marnie she had a lovely coat.

Correct: Marnie had a lovely coat.

Correct: She had a lovely coat.

USAGE   Agreement

Agreement: Pronoun With Antecedent

4.1   A pronoun must agree with its antecedent in number, gender, and person. The antecedent is the noun or noun phrase to which the pronoun refers.

Sentence: *The kittens* chased the mouse. (replace *the kittens* with a pronoun)

Plural antecedent—plural pronoun: *They* chased the mouse.

Sentence: *The boy* flew a kite. (replace *the boy* with a pronoun)

Singular, masculine antecedent—singular, masculine pronoun: *He* flew a kite.

Sentence: *A llama will rush at the attacker and strike with its large feet.* (replace *llama* with a pronoun)

Singular, antecedent—singular, pronoun: *It* will rush at the attacker and strike with its large feet.

Be especially careful to make a possessive pronoun agree with its antecedent.

Correct: An artist is admired for her skill with a brush.

Incorrect: An artist is admired for their skill with a brush.

Agreement: Verb With Subject

4.2   A subject and verb agree if they are both singular or both plural, that is, the subject and verb must agree in number.

Nouns are singular when they refer to one person, place, or thing and plural when they refer to more than one (cat—singular, cats—plural).

Most verbs ending in *s* are singular, while verbs not ending in *s* are plural. The exception to this general rule is verbs used with *I* and singular *you* (which take the same verb form as plural *you)*. Although *I* and *you* are singular, their verbs do not take an *s*: I go, you go, he goes, it goes, they go, we go.

The number of the subject is not affected by any phrases that fall between the subject and the verb. (See "Agreement: Verb With Indefinite Pronoun" on page 75 for the only exception.)

Sentence: The difficulties of going on a long trip were apparent.

Subject: the difficulties (plural)

Verb: were (plural)

The verb should agree with the subject even when the subject and predicate are inverted.

Performing for the first time on this stage are the Lowell sisters. (subject = Lowell sisters, plural verb = are)

Performing for the first time on this stage is Winifred Lowell. (subject = Winifred Lowell, singular verb = is)

Agreement: Verb With Compound Subject

4.3   Compound subjects are formed by joining words or groups of words with *and, or,* or *nor*.

Subjects joined with *and* take a plural verb. This is true whether the words making up the compound subject are singular or plural.

Single subject: Our cat spends a lot of time in the back yard.

Compound subject: Our cat and dog spend a lot of time in the back yard.

Compound subject: Our cats and dogs spend a lot of time in the back yard.

Compound subject: Our cat and dogs spend a lot of time in the back yard.

Compound subject: Our cats and dog spend a lot of time in the back yard.

Note that sometimes *and* is used as part of a phrase that functions as a unit to name a single item. In these cases, the subject is not a compound subject.

Example: Macaroni and cheese is my favorite dish.

Example: Stop and Go was the name of the market.

Singular subjects joined with *or* or *nor* take a singular verb.

Example: A chair or a stool fits under the counter.

Example: Either our cat or our dog sits on the couch.

Example: Neither Melissa nor Jody plays the clarinet.

When plural subjects are joined with *or* or *nor*, they take a plural verb.

Example: Jackets or sweaters are needed in the evenings.

Example: Either his parents or my parents take us to the pool.

Example: Neither our cats nor our dogs like to have baths.

When a plural subject and a singular subject are joined with *or* or *nor*, make the verb agree with the closer of the two subjects.

> Example: A sports coat or evening clothes are required for the dinner party.
>
> Example: Evening clothes or a sports coat is required for the dinner party.
>
> Example: Either my parents or my aunt drives us to school.
>
> Example: Either my aunt or my parents drive us to school.
>
> Example: Neither the secretaries nor the supervisor was happy about the arrangement.
>
> Example: Neither the supervisor nor the secretaries were happy about the arrangement.

Agreement: Verb With Indefinite Pronoun

4.4   The verb must agree with the indefinite pronoun in number. Some of the indefinite pronouns take singular verbs, others take plural verbs, and others vary depending on context.

Singular: another, anybody, anyone, anything, each, each one, either, everybody, everyone, everything, much, neither, nobody, no one, one, other, somebody, someone, something

> Everybody has a car.   Each of the parents has a car.

Plural: both, few, many, several

> Both students have cars.   Several students have cars.

Vary (sometimes singular, sometimes plural): all, any, most, none, some

> Most of the cars were dirty.   Most of the car was dirty.

Note that the indefinite pronouns that can be either singular or plural *(all, any, most, none, some)* constitute an exception to the standard rule of agreement that the number of the subject is not affected by any phrases that fall between the subject and the verb. When *all, any, most, none,* or *some* refer to a singular noun, they take a singular verb. When they refer to a plural noun, they take a plural verb.

> Singular: *Some* of the paper *is* dry.
>
> Plural: *Some* of the papers *are* on the desk.

Agreement: Adjective With Noun/Pronoun

4.5   An adjective and the noun or pronoun it modifies must agree in number.

> She has *two* brothers.

When *this, that, these,* and *those* are used as adjectives, they must agree in number with the noun or pronoun that they are modifying.

> Singular: *this* bird, *that* alligator
>
> Plural: *these* sparrows, *those* crocodiles

Misplaced Modifier

4.6   Modifiers describe, define, clarify, or provide more explicit information about the words they modify. There is nothing intrinsic to the modifiers themselves that shows which word they modify; therefore, modifiers must be carefully placed in sentences so that it is clear which words they modify. Modifiers are said to be misplaced when it is unclear which word they modify or when they modify the wrong word. In general, modifiers should be placed as close as possible to the words they modify. Frequently, misplaced modifiers can be corrected simply by moving the ambiguous phrase closer to the word it modifies.

> Misplaced: I spoke with the woman who is standing by the potted palm in the yellow dress.

In the example above, the reader may think that the palm is draped in a yellow dress. Correct this confusion by relocating the modifier.

> Corrected: I spoke with the woman in the yellow dress who is standing by the potted palm.

Now there is no confusion over who is wearing the yellow dress. In the example below, there is some confusion over who is in the back of the truck.

> Misplaced: He took the dog when he left this morning in the back of the truck.
>
> Correction 1: When he left this morning, he took the dog in the back of the truck.

Now it is clear who is in the back of the truck. There may still be confusion as to whether he took the dog who was already in the back of the truck out of the truck, or he drove the truck as the dog rode in the back.

> Correction 2: When he drove away in the truck this morning, the dog rode in the back.

Now it should be clear that the dog rode.

Unnecessary Words

4.7   Unnecessary words should be deleted.

Negatives: Use only one negative word to state a negative idea.

> Incorrect: We don't have no bananas.
>
> Correct: We don't have any bananas.
>
> Correct: We have no bananas.

The words *hardly* and *scarcely* are also considered negative words and should not be used with other negatives.

> Incorrect: We have hardly no bananas.
>
> Correct: We have hardly any bananas.
>
> Correct: We have no bananas.

Some words are excessive or repetitive and should be deleted. (See also Subject on page 73.)

Incorrect: The thing is is the people are hungry.

Correct: The people are hungry. (or The thing is, the people are hungry.)

Incorrect: Rover he ran away.

Correct: Rover ran away. (or He ran away.)

Special (Confused) Word Pairs

4.8   There are a number of word pairs that are often confused (effect/affect, continually/continuously). In this level of *Editor in Chief®*, we focus on the following frequently confused pairs of words:

bring (to carry something with oneself to a place—from there to here—when you bring something with you, you arrive with it) / take (to carry to another place—from here to there—when you take something with you, you leave with it)

lay (to put or place) / lie (to rest or recline)

leave (to go away) / let (to allow)

may (to be permitted to) / can (to be able to)

raise (to move something to a higher position, to elevate—transitive verb—you raise objects) / rise (to move from lower to higher—intransitive verb—people/objects rise on their own)

teach (to instruct) / learn (to gain knowledge or understanding)

Note: Some words are used incorrectly because of confusion in construction of irregular verb tenses (e.g., I have <u>went</u> instead of I have <u>gone</u> or I <u>went</u>, etc.) See "Verb Tense" on page 69.

PUNCTUATION

Apostrophe

5.1   Use an apostrophe in contractions to show where letters or numbers have been left out.

could not = couldn't   let us = let's   it is = it's

the 1990s = the '90s

5.2   Use an apostrophe to form the plural of letters, but do not use an apostrophe to form the plural of numbers.

Mind your p's and q's.

Shakespeare lived in the late 1500s and early 1600s.

Usage note: At one time, forming the plural of numbers by adding apostrophe *s* was common; however, in current style manuals, the preference is to drop the apostrophe. If you wish to use an apostrophe when forming plural numbers, note that under no circumstances is the construction '90's considered correct.

5.3 Use an apostrophe to form the possessive.

Add *'s* to form the singular possessive.

    dog's bone   Maria's ball   car's color

Add an apostrophe to form the possessive of a plural ending in *-s*, *-es*, or *-ies*.

    cats' toys   foxes' holes   butterflies' flowers

Add *'s* to form the possessive of plural nouns that do not end in *-s*.

    women's hats   sheep's wool   children's toys

Usage notes: Pronouns do not use an apostrophe to form the possessive (see "Personal Pronouns" on page 66). Apostrophes are unnecessary with the regular plurals of words (*the parent<u>s</u> of the boy<u>s</u>*).

Colon

5.4 Use a colon between numbers indicating hours and minutes.

    We will arrive at 9:15.

5.5 A colon follows the greeting in a business letter.

    Dear Sir: Dear Dr. Martinez:

Comma

5.6 Use a comma between words or phrases in a series

    blue, red, and green   up the hill, over the log, and down the hole

Usage note: At one time, including a comma before the *and* in a series was considered optional. This trend has changed. Including the comma is now the preferred pattern of punctuation.

5.7 Use a comma to separate the elements of an address (street and city, city and state). Note: do not use a comma between the state and ZIP code.

    5 Elm Street, Sample Town, New York 13635

5.8 Use a comma after the state (or country) in a sentence when using the format city, state (or city, country; or national park, state, etc.)

    We are going to Sample Town, New York, to visit our grandmother.

    Alexander will be traveling through Paris, France, this summer.

5.9 Use a comma in dates between day and year in the format *month day, year*.

    January 10, 1996   April 5, 2001

Usage note: If you follow the European model, write 9 May 1999—no commas.

5.10 Use a comma after the year in a sentence when using the format *month day, year*.

    We have to be in Nevada on January 10, 1996, in order to visit our friends.

5.11 Use a comma after the greeting of a friendly letter.

Dear Emilio,

Usage note: Business letters use a colon after the salutation (see 5.5).

5.12 Use a comma after the closing of a letter (business or friendly).

Sincerely,   With best wishes,   Love,

5.13 Use commas to separate nouns of address from the rest of the sentence.

Kim, I asked you to step over here.

You know, Rebecca, we could go to the store tomorrow.

5.14 Use a comma to separate an introductory word or interjection from the rest of the sentence.

Yes, I have heard of that TV show.   Hey, did you see that comet?

Well, I guess that's true.

5.15 Use a comma to set off an introductory phrase or dependent clause.

After we left, she phoned the office.

From the couch, the cat jumped onto the bookcase.

Usage note: Dependent clauses are also referred to as subordinate clauses. See "Subordinating Conjunctions" on page 64 for more information.

5.16 Set off a nonessential (nonrestrictive) appositive with commas. (An appositive is a noun or noun/pronoun phrase, next to a noun, that identifies, defines, or explains the noun.) See "Clauses and Punctuation" on page 82 for more on essential/nonessential.

The Marsdens, our nearest neighbors, left on vacation today.

My brother's dog, the big white one, is rolling in the leaves.

5.17 Use commas to set off sentence interrupters.

The recent game, on the other hand, showed the wisdom of working on set plays.

He had told us, however, that he would study more.

5.18 Use commas before coordinating conjunctions joining two independent clauses.

We took the bus, but she will take the train.

My sister mowed the lawn, and I raked the leaves.

He ran outside and shouted to his sister.

Usage note: See "Conjunctions" on page 63 for more information.

5.19 Use a comma to separate a direct quote from a phrase identifying the speaker.

Tomas said, "We had fun doing English today."

"We had fun doing English today," Tomas said.

5.20 Place commas inside ending quotation marks.

The package was marked "fragile," but the contents were quite sturdy.

"We had fun doing English today," Tomas said.

Usage note: We have noted some confusion over this particular rule, possibly because British usage differs from American usage. American style manuals, however, are all in agreement: commas and periods always go inside closing quotation marks.

5.21 Commas are sometimes used inappropriately. Below are some of the more common errors in comma usage. No comma should be used:

Between a subject and its verb.

Incorrect: The chairman of the arts, told the committee to vote.

Between adjectives.

Incorrect: The event was peaceful, and calm.

Between multiple objects of a verb.

Incorrect: She had smooth skin, and tangled hair.

In expressions contrasted through use of correlative conjunctions.

Incorrect: We'll find it not only here, but also there.

With a compound predicate.

Incorrect: The barking dog chased the mailman, and bit him.

With an essential clause.

Incorrect: The manager quit, because she was planning to move.

Incorrect: He mowed the yard, in exchange for a meal.

With compound subjects.

Incorrect: Mr. Darby, and Helen came to town.

Exclamation Point

5.22 Use an exclamation point after an exclamatory sentence.

Stop that dog!   We know what to do!   I love chocolate!

5.23 Use an exclamation point after an interjection that stands alone.

Stop! Don't you know to look both ways before crossing a street?

Usage note: An interjection that begins a sentence may function as an introductory word and be set off from the sentence with a comma instead of an exclamation point. An example might be: Hey, wait for me!

5.24 Place the exclamation point inside quotation marks at the end of a quoted exclamation. (Place it outside when the exclamation applies to the entire sentence.)

Incorrect: "Get that snake off the counter"! screamed Jamie.

Correct: "Get that snake off the counter!" screamed Jamie.

Incorrect: I love my talking "dog!"

Correct: I love my talking "dog"!

Usage note: In contrast to commas and periods (which always fall inside closing quotation marks), an exclamation point falls inside closing quotation marks only when it applies to what is inside the quotation marks. If it is not part of the quoted material, it goes outside the quotation marks; for example, That box is marked "fragile"!

Hyphen

5.25   Use a hyphen with compound numbers.

twenty-five   ninety-four   forty-three

Period

5.26   Use a period to end a declarative sentence.

A sentence begins with a capital letter and ends with a punctuation mark.

5.27   Use a period after abbreviations and initials.

Washington, D.C.   Dr. Nolan   Mr. J. Pedrewski

Note: It is becoming more acceptable to use some common abbreviations without periods, e.g., mph, km, etc. However, for the purposes of consistency in this series, use the periods with abbreviations.

5.28   Always place periods inside closing quotation marks.

We delivered a package marked "fragile."

See usage note under "Comma," section 5.20 on page 80.

Question Mark

5.29   Use a question mark after a direct question (interrogative sentence).

Are we there yet?   What time is it?

5.30   Place a question mark inside the quotation marks after a quoted question but outside the quotation marks when it doesn't apply to the material in quotation marks.

"What day is soccer practice?" asked Lucia.   Did you see "The End of Earth"?

Usage note: Again in contrast to commas and periods (which always fall inside closing quotation marks), a question mark falls inside closing quotation marks only when it applies to what is inside the quotation marks. In the following, the question mark applies to the entire sentence, not the word inside the quotation marks: Is that box marked "fragile"?

Quotation Marks

5.31   Use quotation marks to enclose direct quotes; enclose both parts of a divided quotation. (Do not use quotation marks with indirect quotes.)

"I need help on this English paper," said Grover.

"This beautiful day," said Mark, "is too good to waste indoors."

He said that it was a beautiful day.

5.32   Quotation marks are used to identify the title of a song, story, poem, article, or book chapter.

We have to memorize "Jabberwocky" by Thursday.

Clauses and Punctuation

Recognizing dependent and independent clauses is useful when punctuating sentences. In some instances, commas are required between dependent and independent clauses, and in other cases, they are not. Following are a few simple rules of thumb for when to use commas in sentences containing clauses:

5.33   independent clause + independent clause =

comma after the first clause when the clauses are joined by a coordinating conjunction

Example: The sun was shining brightly, and the weather was warm.

5.34   independent clause + independent clause =

semicolon after the first clause when the clauses are not joined by a coordinating conjunction

Example: The sun was shining brightly; the weather was warm.

5.35   dependent clause + independent clause =

comma after the dependent clause

Example: After we left for the country, the package we were waiting for arrived.

5.36   independent clause + dependent clause =

varies depending on whether the dependent clause is essential (restrictive) or nonessential (nonrestrictive)

Essential (restrictive) clauses are essential to the meaning of the sentence. Removing them would change the meaning of the sentence. Nonessential (nonrestrictive) clauses can be removed without altering the meaning of the sentence. Nonessential clauses give additional or incidental information; they are not essential to the basic idea that the sentence is conveying.

Essential: The man who is sitting in that chair by the wall is our neighbor.

Nonessential: Our neighbor, who is sitting in that chair by the wall, is well-liked in our community.

Usage note: The only nonessential clause used at this level of *Editor in Chief*® is the appositive (a noun or noun/pronoun phrase, next to a noun, that identifies, defines, or explains the noun).

A sentence will not contain two dependent clauses without an independent clause.

To aid in remembering the rules for punctuating clauses, think of them as follows:

I + I = comma

I + D = no comma

D + I = comma

Note that the rules above apply to clauses, not phrases. For more on the difference between clauses and phrases, see pages 71–73.

Run-On Sentences

5.37   In this level of *Editor in Chief*®, the answer key corrects run-on sentences by creating two sentences: the first ending in a period and the second beginning with a capital letter. Although in the answers we do not provide all the alternatives listed below, you may wish to correct the run-on sentences using a semicolon or conjunction.

Incorrect: One sea lion balanced a ball another sea lion waved his flipper.

Incorrect: One sea lion balanced a ball, another sea lion waved his flipper.

Correct: One sea lion balanced a ball. Another sea lion waved his flipper.

Correct: One sea lion balanced a ball; another sea lion waved his flipper.

Correct: One sea lion balanced a ball, and another sea lion waved his flipper.

Sentence Fragments

5.38 In this level of *Editor in Chief*®, the answer key corrects sentence fragments by joining the sentence fragment to a complete sentence.

Incorrect: The bird was sitting on the roof. Sunning himself.

Correct: The bird was sitting on the roof sunning himself.

Note that a sentence fragment may also be corrected by rewriting the sentence in other ways, as shown below. We leave this to your discretion.

Possible: Sunning himself, the bird sat on the roof.

SPELLING

Homophones...and other "Sound Alikes"

6.1 In this level of *Editor in Chief*®, we focus on the following homophones:

are/our

ceiling/sealing   to/too/two

in to/into   where/were

its/it's   whose/who's

lose/loose   your/you're

secrets/secretes

their/they're/there

Plurals

6.2 Some words have the same form for the singular and plural.

sheep   deer   bison

6.3 The plurals of words that end in the sound of *f* are usually formed by changing the *f* to *v* and adding *-es*.

leaf/leaves   knife/knives

6.4 The plurals of words that end in *y* are usually formed by changing the *y* to *i* and adding *-es*.

berry/berries

Possessives

See "Apostrophe" on page 77.

Special Usage Problems

6.5 could of/could have: *could of* should not be used for *could have*; *of* should not be used for *have*

a lot: *a lot* is always two words

Note: Some words can be spelled in more than one way. For example, both of the following are correct:

toward   towards

READING DETECTIVE® SAMPLE ACTIVITY

On the following pages is a sample activity from our popular reading series, *Reading Detective*®. There are currently four books in the series: *Reading Detective*® *Beginning,* (Grades 3–4), *Reading Detective*® A1, (Grades 5–6), *Reading Detective*® B1, (Grades 7–8), and *Reading Detective*® *Rχ* (Grades 6-12). The Beginning, A1, and B1 levels of *Reading Detective*® are also available as software. The following sample is from the B1 book.

• *Reading Detective* ® is based on national and state reading standards. These books, however, go beyond current reading comprehension materials by requiring a higher level of analysis and evidence to support answers. Students are asked to read a passage, then answer a variety of questions, supporting their answers with specific evidence from the passage. This skill, required by most state standards, is not often addressed in the available reading materials.

• Skills covered include basic reading skills such as reading for detail and identifying the main idea, literary analysis skills such as analyzing character traits and identifying setting, and critical thinking skills such as making inferences and distinguishing between cause and effect.

• Each book includes excerpts from works of award-winning authors and original fiction in a variety of genres: mystery, fantasy, adventure, and humor. Nonfiction articles cover topics in science, social studies, math, and the arts that coincide with classroom curriculum.

• For further samples and information on the *Reading Detective*® series, see our web site at www.CriticalThinking.com.

20. Old Woman of the Oak
by Margaret Hockett

A [1]I crossed the stream, wound my way through the bushes, and came to a clearing. [2]The oak sprawled before me.

B [3]I pressed a dark knot on the pale gray trunk. [4]A rope ladder immediately snaked its way down through rustling red leaves. [5]A note had been tacked to the third rung: CAREFUL, JUDE. ROPE WET. [6]That was Old Meg, never one to waste words.

C [7]Soon, I was swinging my legs into the entrance. [8]Meg sat in her "living room" in the oak she called home. [9]She was as gnarled as the tree, but her eyes usually crackled with fire. [10]Today they were flat.

D [11]"Won't be much longer," she said. [12]"They're going to bulldoze the field for the new road."

E [13]"No way!" I said in disbelief. [14]"We'll stop them—" [15]She held up her hand.

F [16]"But where will you go…?" I started.

G [17]She was moving her rocker back,

baack, baaack—until it was on the edge of the runner and you thought she was going all the way over!—and then forward. [18]She'd do that when she was making up her mind.

H [19]"Been here 'bout long enough. [20]Seen the sun set nine thousand times, and ain't none of them been the same as the one before." [21]I followed her gaze past dewy leaves, a patch of meadow, and jutting rocks of the coast. [22]An inky line was forming a boundary between sea and sky. [23]Suddenly, it spread, as if an artist were washing the scene with a dark tint. [24]My mood darkened with it as Meg's meaning came home to me.

I [25]"I'm leaving you my Oak Log," she announced. [26]Her precious journal! [27]Meg thought the road project was a sign that her time had come, that her life was over! [28]I couldn't accept that.

J [29]As I walked back to town, I ignored the slapping branches, the wet stream, and the cold night. [30]I was making a plan.

6. Jude is most likely to make a plan to
   A. force Meg to move.
   B. move in with Meg.
   C. get the Oak Log.
   D. stop the bulldozing.

   List the numbers of the 2 sentences that best support your answer. ____,

   ____

10. In sentence 24, what does Jude infer from Meg's comments?

    _____

    _____

    _____

    Give the number of the sentence that confirms Jude's inference. ____

SAMPLE ANSWERS

2. Paragraph B suggests that Meg's speech is (character trait)

   A. brief.

   B. lengthy.

   C. mean.

   D. descriptive.

   Give 1 evidence sentence: **6**

3. In sentence 9, "gnarled" most likely means (vocabulary)

   A. hard.

   B. twisted.

   C. tall.

   D. awesome.

   Since "gnarled" is contrasted with the liveliness of her eyes, the author probably wants to show that Meg's body is aged, as a tree with knots and twisted branches.

4. Why did Jude need to be careful in climbing to Meg's home? (reading for detail)

   The rope was wet.

6. Jude is most likely to make a plan to (predict outcome)

   A. force Meg to move.

   B. move in with Meg.

   C. get the Oak Log.

   D. stop the bulldozing.

   List 2 evidence sentences: **13, 14**

   Choice D is supported by sentences 13 and 14, which show that Jude has strong feelings against the bulldozing. B is unlikely because there is no evidence that moving in with Meg would help. Since Meg is already going to give Jude the Oak Log, C is incorrect. A is a possibility but is unsupported.

10. In sentence 24, what does Jude infer from Meg's comments? (inference)

    He probably infers that Meg thinks her time has come to leave or die or both.

    Give 1 evidence sentence: **27**